the new kosher

Simple Recipes to Savor & Share

KIM KUSHNER

For Milan, Emanuel, and Rafaela

photography
KATE SEARS

weldon**owen**

contents

introduction

I don't always love to cook. That is the simple truth.

Because I write cookbooks and teach cooking classes for a living, most people assume that I must really love cooking. But here is the reality: My life, much like yours, is not a dream world. When I serve dinner, no candles are lit, no opera is playing in the background. It's not like it is in the pasta commercials. I'm not perfectly made up—no fresh lipstick or rosy cheeks.

When I'm at home cooking, about fifty other things are going on around me at the same time. Usually this includes my boisterous sons playing football in the middle of our New York City apartment and my daughter, in her *Frozen* tutu, running up and down the hallway while dragging her Hello Kitty rolling suitcase that is cascading musical instruments, stuffed animals, and candy in a trail along the floor. A loud siren is typically sounding outdoors. It's probably a fire truck, and a squad of firefighters is likely gathered around the building next door, where there seems to be some mysterious pipe issues. Of course, the phone is ringing off the hook, too.

My life is not very different from yours. We are all busy. Life is always hectic. Stuff is going on continuously, even when you're cooking dinner. So there you have it.

Perhaps if I could cook all of my meals holed up in a rustic rural kitchen that overlooks beautiful mountains, a crackling fire in the fireplace, and John Legend blasting in the background, I would always love cooking. There I would have the time to coddle my bubbling cast-iron pots of slow-braised meats and hand-picked vegetables while waiting for my tall, dark, and handsome husband to walk through the front door (well, he actually does exist). But that's not how my cooking happens, so I don't love it all the time.

Let me tell you what I do love. It is what comes after the cooking part. I love sitting around the table with the people whom I love (and scream at) the most: my family, my friends, my neighbors. I love eating good food, tasting delicious flavors, drinking wine, laughing, learning, connecting. I love the way time stops in those moments, and how I always forget about the cooking part. The sound of clinking glasses, the smiles on people's faces, the movement. The way my

husband closes his eyes and grins after he takes that first bite. Watching my boys tear their challah into tiny pieces and dip it into the leftover sauce streaked on their plates. Staring at my daughter's chubby fingers stuffing the food into her mouth with satisfaction. To me, nothing is more gratifying than these moments. And that is why I cook.

I was raised in a modern Orthodox home in a vibrant kosher community in Montreal and first learned to cook from my mother, who was born in Morocco and grew up in Israel. My mother's life revolves around food, and her generosity through her love of feeding other people has been the greatest influence on my cooking.

We ate family style, starting with soup and sturdy Moroccan-style meze-like platters of various dishes—hummus, tomato salads, avocado mixtures, lots of variations on eggplant—that we would pass around. A spicy fish dish followed as a first course and then came the meat as a main. I find myself repeating these recipes, though somehow mine are a little more modern.

I always knew how to cook because I grew up cooking. As soon as I moved to New York City and got a place of my own, I started hosting dinner parties. I later attended the Institute of Culinary Education in Manhattan, but it's never been about achieving perfection in the kitchen—only about creating comfort and happiness.

At home, I don't believe in plating the food I serve. My house is not a fine-dining restaurant; it is my home. My guests are not my customers; they are my family and friends. My kitchen is not the center of my business; my kitchen is the center of my heart. When I think about food, many strong memories and traditions from my upbringing filter into everything I make. I express myself through my food. Cooking serves as a connector, a comfort in my life.

I feed the people I love the kind of food I love to eat. And that's what you will find in this book. All of the recipes are straightforward, approachable, and simple to make. Many of them require fewer than six ingredients. They are all tried-and-true.

> The first chapter is titled Kim's Essentials because, to be frank, that's what they are. These recipes are my go-to foods, the ones I always have on hand, including Addictive Pickled Carrots & Radishes with Indian Spices, and Lazy Crumb Topping. They are the items that I can whip up in minutes, like Homemade Pita Chips with Za'atar Chips and 5-Minute Sun-Dried Tomato Hummus. Here is where you'll also find my favorite sauces, dips, crumbs, cookies, and challah—my essentials.

The book then follows traditional menu categories, with each chapter filled with mouthwatering, quick-and-easy recipes for every day. Tiny plates and bite-sized spoonfuls of artistically garnished culinary masterpieces are not my thing. I like to dig in when I eat. I want to bite into my food and savor it.

Through this book, I am inviting you to sit at my table and uncover the recipes from my home. As you turn the pages, you'll see a mix of bowls and platters, of different shapes and sizes, of big spoons and little spoons. My food is often served with spoons. I offer many dips and other mezes; little bowls of salad, such as melt-in-your-mouth eggplant, crisp latkes, and butternut squash chips. I include huge salads, too, like shredded kale with crisp, colorful radishes and a crunchy fresh-off-the-cob corn salad with baby tomatoes. You'll find a baking dish flaunting golden crumb–topped flounder and glass bowls filled to the brim with pasta with fresh tomato sauce or pomegranate-studded quinoa. And I must not forget to mention the wineglasses constantly being refilled with gorgeous reds and whites.

These beautiful, vibrant foods sit right before your eyes, waiting to be passed from hand to hand, like a chain linking one person to the next, until they find their way back to the center of the table. At my house, we eat as a family, family style. The spills and stains on my tablecloths prove it.

If you're Jewish but don't keep kosher or if you're not Jewish at all, you may be wondering, what's in this book for me? Let me ask you, do you enjoy serving amazing food to your family and friends—dishes that are a snap to prepare and are made with wholesome ingredients? If so, this book is for you. Okay, so you won't find any recipes for bacon and shellfish here. But I promise that you'll find lots to love.

P.S. On Being Kosher

People often ask me if I feel deprived keeping a kosher diet. Look, I have steamed lobsters and rendered pancetta in extraordinary Manhattan restaurants beyond my front door. Trust me, I know what I am missing out on. But still, I don't regret my choice to abide by the Jewish dietary laws. In fact, I think that keeping kosher actually creates more of a hunger (pardon the pun) in me to prepare the absolute best dishes that I can. My dietary restrictions inspire me to use the ingredients that I can eat to create beautiful and delicious meals. I don't look at keeping kosher as what I can't eat, but rather what I can.

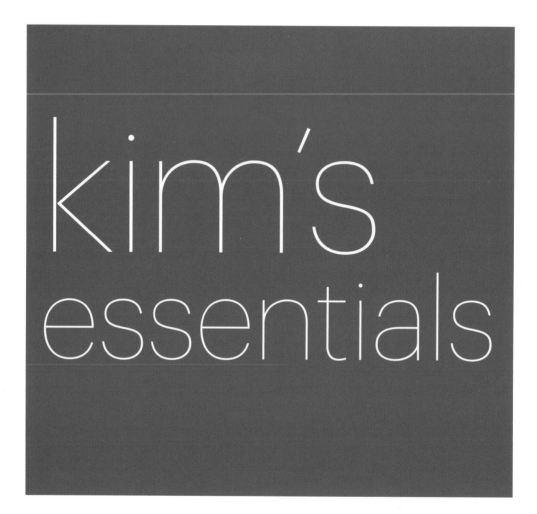

best-ever yogurt dipping sauce

Thick and creamy Greek yogurt works splendidly as the base for a dipping sauce that goes well with many fish and vegetable dishes. My favorite pairing is with the roasted eggplant and onion recipe on page 163. I use parsley and mint in the version here, though you can swap them out for nearly any fresh herbs. The pomegranate seeds add color, crunch, and juiciness. This sauce takes just minutes to make, and I'm willing to bet that at least one person you know will try eating it by the spoonful.

1	cup (8 oz/250 g) plain Greek yogurt
2	tablespoons finely chopped fresh flat-leaf parsley
1	tablespoon finely chopped fresh mint, plus whole leaves for garnish
	Juice of 1 lemon
	Kosher salt and freshly ground black pepper
	Seeds of 1 pomegranate
2	tablespoons *silan* (date syrup)
1	teaspoon red pepper flakes (optional)

In a small bowl, stir together the yogurt, parsley, chopped mint, and lemon juice. Season with salt and black pepper. Stir in the pomegranate seeds. Drizzle with the *silan*, sprinkle with the red pepper flakes, if using, and garnish with whole mint leaves. It's best to prepare this dish just before serving, as it gets watery over time.

Serves 4–6

homemade pita chips with za'atar

My friends are always popping in to say hello and have a drink. This is a great recipe for a five-minute appetizer. I serve these toasty, salty pita chips alongside hummus and guacamole, and they're also a wonderful accompaniment to wine and cheese. I simply top the pitas with a drizzle of olive oil and a sprinkle of za'atar before toasting them in a hot oven. Za'atar is a Middle Eastern spice blend that typically includes oregano, thyme, savory, and sumac, along with toasted sesame seeds and salt. I use it a lot in my cooking because of its sharp, nutty taste. This recipe is a perfect example of when homemade just completely crushes the store-bought equivalent. I keep bags of pita in my freezer in case I need to whip these chips up quickly. They're light, crisp, and delicious, and everyone seems to love them, especially the kids!

4	pita breads
¼	cup (2 fl oz/60 ml) extra-virgin olive oil
1–2	tablespoons za'atar

Preheat the oven to 375°F (190°C).

Split each pita bread horizontally along the outside edge and separate into 2 rounds. Place the rounds, cut side down, on a baking sheet. Drizzle the oil over the pita rounds and sprinkle with the za'atar.

Bake until lightly toasted, about 5 minutes, watching the rounds closely as they can burn quickly. Let cool, then break into smaller pieces and serve. The pita chips will keep in an airtight container at room temperature for up to 1 week.

Makes about 32 chips

5-minute sun-dried tomato hummus

This is a play on the five-minute hummus recipe that appeared in my first cookbook, *The Modern Menu*. It received so much praise that I started playing around with the idea of infusing new flavors into the buzz-worthy recipe. Here, I add not only sun-dried tomatoes to the hummus but also the oil in which the tomatoes are packed, plus some white wine for zest. Not long ago, I declared to a group of friends that I eat hummus every day. And it's absolutely true. With a recipe as foolproof as this one, why wouldn't I?

2	cans (15 oz/470 g each) chickpeas (I use organic), drained and rinsed
2	cloves garlic
6	drained oil-packed sun-dried tomatoes (reserve the oil)
¼	cup (2 fl oz/60 ml) sun-dried tomato oil
1	heaping tablespoon tahini
2	teaspoons dry white wine
	Kosher salt and freshly ground pepper
	Olive oil for drizzling (optional)

In a food processor, combine the chickpeas, garlic, sun-dried tomatoes, tomato oil, and tahini and pulse until thoroughly combined. While continuing to pulse, gradually add the wine, 1 teaspoon at a time, through the feed tube, then continue to pulse until the desired consistency is reached. Season generously with salt and pepper.

Transfer the hummus to a serving dish. Or, if not serving right away, transfer to an airtight container and drizzle olive oil over the hummus to help it stay moist. The hummus will keep in the fridge for up to 2 weeks.

Makes about 2 cups (1 lb/500 g)

curry-spiced mixed seeds

These delicious, tangy seeds are hard to resist. Sprinkle them on soups and salads, such as the shredded romaine salad on page 87, or enjoy them on their own as a healthy snack.

½	cup (2 oz/60 g) unsalted sunflower seeds
½	cup (2 oz/60 g) unsalted pumpkin seeds
2	tablespoons neutral oil, such as grapeseed or rice bran
2	tablespoons curry powder
2	teaspoons sugar
1	teaspoon dry mustard
1	teaspoon cayenne pepper
	Kosher salt and freshly ground black pepper

Preheat the oven to 350°F (180°C).

In a large bowl, toss together the sunflower seeds, pumpkin seeds, oil, curry powder, sugar, mustard, cayenne, and ½ teaspoon each salt and black pepper until well combined. Pour the seed mixture onto a baking sheet and spread evenly.

Roast until toasted, about 10 minutes. Let cool completely before serving. The seeds will keep in a tightly capped glass jar at room temperature for up to 1 month.

Makes about 1 cup (4 oz/125 g)

butternut squash chips with herbes de provence

This is one of those recipes you're going to want to memorize and make time and time again. Whenever I bring out a bowl of these golden, crispy chips, my guests go crazy for them. Herbes de Provence is a mild blend that commonly includes rosemary, thyme, oregano, marjoram, savory, and sometimes lavender. You can find it in the spices aisle at pretty much any supermarket.

1	butternut squash, about 2 lb (1 kg), peeled, halved, and seeded
3	tablespoons extra-virgin olive oil
1–2	tablespoons herbes de Provence
	Kosher salt and freshly ground pepper

Preheat the oven to 375°F (190°C). Line 2 baking sheets with parchment paper.

Use a sharp knife or a mandoline to cut the butternut squash into thin slices.

Transfer the slices to a large bowl and drizzle with the oil. Sprinkle with the herbes de Provence, 1 teaspoon salt, and ½ teaspoon pepper. Toss to coat evenly.

Transfer the squash to the prepared baking sheets. Try to spread the slices in a single layer. Roast for 20 minutes, then reduce the oven temperature to 350°F (180°C) and roast until they begin to curl, about 30 minutes longer. Let cool, then break into smaller pieces and serve. The chips will keep in an airtight container in the refrigerator for up to 1 week.

Serves 6–8

addictive pickled carrots & radishes with indian spices

Imagine bright, crisp carrots and radishes pickled in a sweet but spicy brine that take just minutes to prepare. That's what this recipe is all about. I love using multicolored carrots, as the colors intensify over time. Instead of the typical pickling spices, I infuse Indian flavors into these vegetables. The bold coriander seeds are a perfect match for the deep barbecue flavors of the tandoori masala powder. Both the seeds and the spice mix can be found in specialty-food shops and online.

12	small organic carrots with tops, trimmed with 1 inch (2.5 cm) of the stem intact and peeled
12	organic radishes with tops, trimmed with 1 inch (2.5 cm) of the stem intact
1	lemon
½	cup (4 fl oz/125 ml) cider vinegar
½	cup (4 fl oz/125 ml) rice vinegar
3	tablespoons sugar
	Kosher salt
1	tablespoon tandoori masala powder
1	teaspoon coriander seeds

Rinse and dry the carrots and radishes well. Cut some or all of the carrots and radishes in half lengthwise, if you like. Wash and dry a glass jar with a wide opening (I use an empty jam or coffee jar).

Cut the lemon in half and squeeze the juice into a small saucepan; reserve the lemon halves. Add the vinegars, sugar, 3 tablespoons salt, the masala powder, and coriander seeds. Stir with a wooden spoon and bring the mixture to a boil over high heat, 1–2 minutes. Remove from the heat and let cool for 10 minutes.

Pack the carrots, radishes, and reserved lemon halves into the jar and pour in the brine. The vegetables should be fully submerged. If they are not, add equal parts cider and rice vinegar as needed to cover. Cover with the lid and refrigerate for at least 3 hours or up to 3 weeks. The longer the vegetables stand, the stronger the flavor, but I like mine even after just an hour or two of standing. Warning: these are addictive.

Makes about one 1-pint (500-ml) jar

puff pastry twists

This is the easiest recipe in the book. If you're having company and want to put out something savory, warm, and crisp—and that will also fill your home with the most amazing aroma—this recipe is for you. And if you're looking to serve a treat that's sweet, delicate, and perfect with a cup of coffee or a bowl of sorbet, this recipe is for you, too. I brush store-bought puff pastry sheets with an egg wash, melted butter, or olive oil; sprinkle them with intense sweet or savory flavor combos; cut them into long strips; and twist them into long spirals. I bake them until they are golden and fragrant and then display them in tall glasses. They are showstoppers and are devoured in no time. These twists look great on my table at cocktail or dinner parties and are always a hit at Yom Kippur break-fast. Best of all, I prepare them in advance and freeze them unbaked on baking sheets. Then, just before my guests arrive, I transfer them straight from the freezer to a preheated oven and voilà: hot, crisp, golden twists for the table.

| 1 | sheet frozen puff pastry (I use Pepperidge Farm), partially thawed on the countertop for 15 minutes |
| 1 | large egg, beaten |

For the Za'atar & Truffle Topping
| 1 | tablespoon za'atar |
| ½ | teaspoon truffle salt |

For the Sesame, Parmesan & Garlic Topping
2	tablespoons black sesame seeds
3	tablespoons grated Parmesan cheese
1	teaspoon garlic powder

For the Vanilla Sugar & Cinnamon Topping
| 3 | tablespoons Vanilla Bean Sugar (page 37) |
| 1 | teaspoon ground cinnamon |

Preheat the oven to 400°F (200°C). Line a baking sheet with parchment paper.

Place the puff pastry on another piece of parchment paper. Roll out gently into a rectangle about 14 by 9 inches (35 by 23 cm). Brush the egg wash evenly over the top surface of the pastry. In a small bowl, stir together the topping ingredients of your choice and sprinkle evenly over the pastry. Use a sharp knife to cut the pastry crosswise into strips about 1 inch (2.5 cm) wide. Working with 1 strip at a time, grasp each end with one hand and twist gently in opposite directions to form a spiral. As the pastries are formed, place them on the prepared baking sheet.

Bake until the twists are golden, about 10 minutes. Serve at room temperature or store at room temperature in an airtight container for up to 1 week.

If not baking right away, cover the unbaked twists with plastic wrap and freeze for up to 30 days. Then bake the frozen twists in a preheated 400°F (200°C) oven for about 12 minutes.

Makes 12–15 twists

vanilla bean applesauce

Here is a popular fall staple. This luscious, silky applesauce is scented with vanilla bean. Keep a jar of it in the fridge at all times. It's delicious on its own or served alongside roasted potatoes or even sliced brisket, and both kids and adults love it. It is simple to make, too, and no store-bought competitor can beat it for flavor and texture.

10–15 apples (any variety), 3½–4 lb (1.75–2 kg) total weight, peeled, quartered, and cored

1 vanilla bean, split lengthwise

In a large pot, combine the apples, vanilla bean, and ¼ cup (2 fl oz/60 ml) water and bring to a boil over high heat. Reduce the heat to medium, cover, and cook for 35–50 minutes without stirring. (The water will prevent the apples from scorching.) The timing will depend on how many apples you use: The more fruit, the longer the mixture will need to cook. To test for doneness, pierce the apples with a fork. They should be extremely soft and almost falling apart.

Carefully remove the vanilla bean from the pot and let it cool for a few minutes. Then, using the tip of a sharp knife, scrape the seeds into the pot and discard the pod.

Let the apple mixture cool for about 5 minutes longer. If you prefer a smooth applesauce, transfer the mixture, in batches, to a food processor, and pulse until smooth. If you prefer a chunky sauce, use a potato masher to mash the fruit to your desired consistency. Let cool completely, then transfer to one or more glass jars. The applesauce will keep in the fridge for up to 2 weeks.

Makes 3–4 cups (27–36 oz/845 g–1.1 kg)

perfect challah

Challah is simple to make, but it does take time. If you're willing to give over a day to baking these loaves, however, you will be amply rewarded. Once the dough is prepared, it requires two risings before it is shaped into loaves, brushed with egg wash, sprinkled with toppings, and baked. It's delicious eaten warm right out of the oven. The cooled loaves can be wrapped in plastic wrap, placed in lock-top plastic bags, and frozen for up to 6 weeks. But they are hard to resist, so I doubt that they will last that long.

4	packages active dry yeast
2	cups (1 lb/500 g) sugar
4	cups (32 fl oz/1 l) warm (but not hot) water
¾	cup (6 fl oz/180 ml) canola oil
6	large eggs
¼	cup (3 oz/90 g) honey, plus 1 teaspoon
	Kosher salt
1	bag (5 lb/2.5 kg) bread flour
	Sesame seeds, Sweet Crumb Topping (page 32), Za'atar Everything Topping (page 33), or topping of choice

Preheat the oven to 200°F (95°C). When the oven reaches that temperature, turn it off.

In a bowl, stir together the yeast, sugar, and warm water. Place the bowl in the warm oven. After a few minutes, the yeast will start bubbling and form a frothy mixture.

Meanwhile, in a very large bowl, combine the oil, 4 of the eggs, the ¼ cup honey, and 2¼ teaspoons salt and stir until combined. Remove the yeast mixture from the oven and stir it into the egg mixture. Pour in half of the flour and mix with your hands. Add the remaining flour and combine well with your hands. The dough should be thick, somewhat sticky, and even a little lumpy. Cover the bowl with a kitchen towel and let the dough rise at room temperature until doubled, 4–6 hours.

Once the dough has risen, divide it evenly into tennis ball–sized portions.

To make braided challahs, line 3 large baking sheets with parchment paper. Roll 3 of the dough balls into "snakes," each 10 inches (25 cm) long. Braid them (just the way you'd braid hair) and pinch and turn under the ends to secure. Repeat with the remaining dough balls. Place 2 challahs on each of the prepared baking sheets, spacing them 3 inches (7.5 cm) apart. Cover the loaves with a kitchen towel and let rise until swelled, 2–4 hours.

To make pull-apart challahs, lightly grease a 9- or 10-inch (23- or 25-cm) round cake pan. Place a dough ball in the center of the pan and surround with more balls to fill the pan. The balls should be close but not touching (they will rise and eventually touch). Cover the dough with a kitchen towel and let rise until swelled, 2–4 hours. Repeat with the remaining dough balls. You will need several round cake pans to create only pull-apart challahs. I like to mix and match, making some braided and some pull-apart loaves. That way, I am sure to have enough baking sheets and cake pans!

Preheat the oven to 350°F (180°C).

In a small bowl, whisk together the remaining 2 eggs and 1 teaspoon honey. Once the challahs have risen, brush them with the egg wash and sprinkle generously with a topping. Working in batches that will comfortably fit in your oven, bake the loaves until golden, rotating the pans 180 degrees halfway throughout baking. (I bake 3 challahs at a time in a convection oven set at 325°F/165°C.) Transfer the loaves to wire racks and let cool.

Makes 5–7 loaves, depending on size and shape

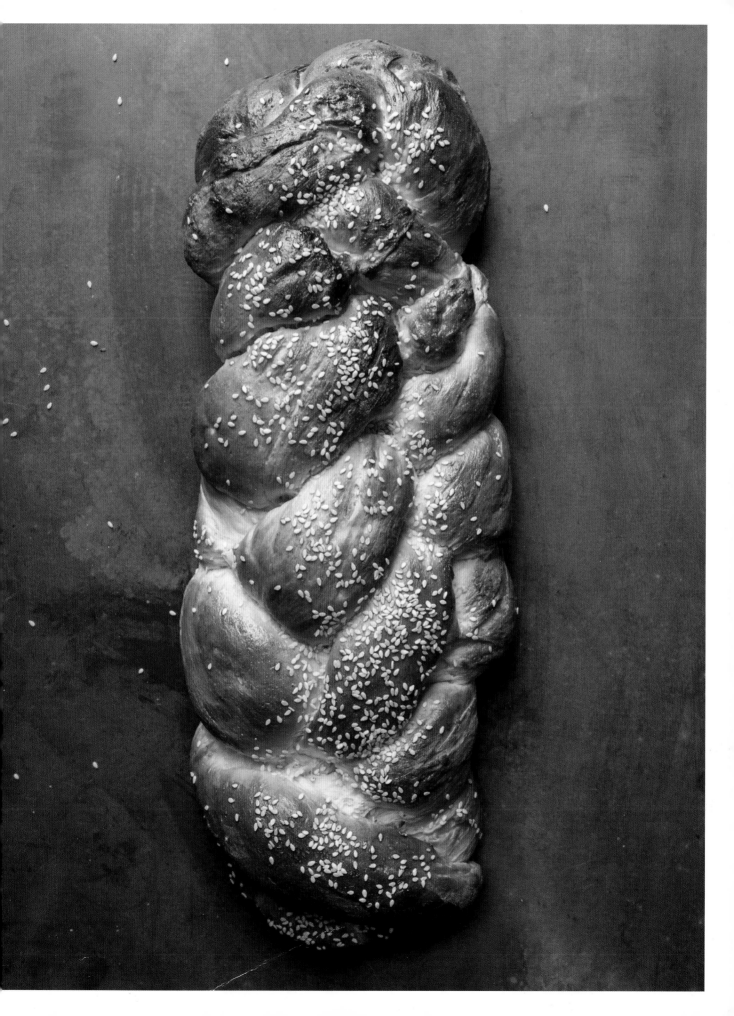

sweet crumb topping

This divine sweet topping is made using the tiny seeds found inside a vanilla bean pod—in other words, real vanilla. It is fantastic strewn over challah (page 30): brush the risen loaves with egg wash as directed, then sprinkle the topping evenly over them.

1	cup (5 oz/155 g) all-purpose flour
1	cup (8 oz/250 g) sugar
6	tablespoons (3 fl oz/90 ml) canola oil
1	vanilla bean

In a bowl, combine the flour, sugar, and oil. Use a sharp knife to split the vanilla bean open lengthwise, then use the knife tip to scrape the seeds into the bowl. Use your fingers to incorporate the ingredients to form a nice crumbly topping. The topping will keep in an airtight container at room temperature for up to 1 month.

Makes 2¼ cups (1 lb/500 g)

spicy maple crumb topping

Sprinkle this topping over just about any vegetable before roasting. My favorites are brussels sprouts and sweet potatoes. You will never look at maple syrup the same way again!

½	cup (2 oz/60 g) cornflake crumbs
¼	cup (3 oz/90 g) pure maple syrup
1	fresh or dried sage leaf
¼	teaspoon red pepper flakes

In a mini food processor, combine the cornflake crumbs, maple syrup, sage leaf, and red pepper flakes. Process until the ingredients are combined and the mixture is crumbly, like sand. The topping will keep in an airtight container at room temperature for up to 2 weeks.

Makes about ½ cup (5 oz/155 g)

za'atar everything topping

If you're looking to spice up your homemade challahs (page 30), this is the topping for you. It has everything you're sure to like—it's salty, nutty, garlicky, and crunchy—and it's easy to use: just brush the risen loaves with egg wash as directed, then sprinkle the topping evenly over them. It's also terrific on basmati rice, grilled fish, and roasted vegetables.

½	cup (2¼ oz/70 g) za'atar
1	tablespoon garlic powder
1	tablespoon sesame seeds
1	tablespoon poppy seeds
1	teaspoon caraway seeds

In a small bowl, stir together the za'atar, garlic powder, sesame seeds, poppy seeds, and caraway seeds. The topping will keep in an airtight container at room temperature for up to 6 months.

Makes about ⅔ cup (2½ oz/70 g)

lazy crumb topping

This is the ultimate go-to crumb topping. Prepare it in advance and store it in the fridge for up to 2 weeks, so you'll have it on hand, ready to go. That way, making dinner will be a snap, which is why I call it my "lazy" crumb topping. Use it to coat fish fillets (page 103) or sprinkle it over a whole side of your favorite fish. It's perfect for breaded chicken, too. The addition of sun-dried tomatoes and lemon zest makes these crumbs memorable.

¼   cup (1 oz/30 g) cornflake crumbs
⅓   cup (¾ oz/20 g) panko
3   drained oil-packed sun-dried tomatoes, chopped
        Zest and juice of ½ lemon
        Kosher salt and freshly ground pepper

In a mini food processor, combine the cornflake crumbs, panko, sun-dried tomatoes, and lemon zest and juice. Process until the ingredients are combined and the mixture is crumbly. Season well with salt and pepper. Taste the crumbs and adjust the seasoning as needed. The crumb topping will keep in an airtight container in the fridge for up to 2 weeks.

Makes about 1 cup (3 oz/90 g)

perfect graham cracker crumbs

I keep a container of these crumbs in my refrigerator at all times as they're great for throwing together a last-minute dessert, like individual sorbet or ice cream parfaits. Just sprinkle a teaspoon of these buttery, crunchy crumbs into a champagne or martini glass, add a scoop or two of your favorite frozen treat, and sprinkle a few more crumbs over the top. They're a key ingredient in my Deconstructed S'mores (page 185), and I also like to spoon them over sliced bananas or stir them into my yogurt. What could be better?

1¾	cups (5¼ oz/160 g) graham cracker crumbs (about 20 graham crackers, ground in a food processor)
2	tablespoons all-purpose flour
2	tablespoons sugar
	Kosher salt
½	cup (4 oz/125 g) unsalted butter, melted and cooled

Preheat the oven to 350°F (180°C).

In a bowl, combine the graham cracker crumbs, flour, sugar, and a pinch of salt. Stir in the butter and then combine thoroughly using a spoon or your hands. Spread the mixture out in an even layer on a baking sheet.

Bake the crumbs until golden, about 10 minutes. Let cool completely before using. The crumbs will keep in an airtight container in the fridge for up to 1 month.

Makes about 2 cups (6 oz/185 g)

vanilla bean sugar

Here is one of my pantry staples. Burying a split vanilla bean in a jar of granulated sugar creates an awesome vanilla-scented sugar that I often use in place of regular sugar in baking recipes. It is also wonderful dusted over French toast (page 45) and Puff Pastry Twists (page 28) or sprinkled atop cookies, cakes, and fresh fruits.

2	cups (1 lb/500 g) sugar
1	vanilla bean, split lengthwise

Place the sugar in a glass jar and stick the vanilla bean into the center. Cover with a tight-fitting lid and store at room temperature. The longer the sugar stands, the more intense the vanilla flavor. The sugar will keep for months!

Makes 2 cups (1 lb/500 g)

happy cookies

You might be wondering why there's a cookie recipe at this point in the book. Well here's why: This is my absolute go-to recipe for cookies. There's nothing like the perfect sugar cookie, and these explode with bright colors from the sprinkles that are folded into the dough, putting a smile on everyone's face. I call them my "happy cookies," and I keep a batch of the dough in my freezer at all times. A plate of these treats makes a great gift or snack—they are perfect with a cup of coffee or a glass of milk.

¾	cup (6 oz/185 g) unsalted butter, at room temperature
1	cup (8 oz/250 g) sugar
4	large eggs
2	teaspoons vanilla extract
	Kosher salt
3½	cups (17½ oz/540 g) all-purpose flour
½	cup (3 oz/90 g) colored sprinkles

In a stand mixer fitted with the whisk attachment, beat together the butter and sugar on high speed until creamy, about 2 minutes. Add 3 of the eggs, one at a time, beating on high speed after each addition until combined. Add the vanilla and beat until combined, about 2 minutes longer. Switch to the paddle attachment and add 1 teaspoon salt and then add the flour, ½ cup (2½ oz/75 g) at a time, beating on medium speed until the dough is soft and holds together without being sticky. Add the flour gradually to achieve a smooth dough (you may not need all of it). Stir in the sprinkles.

Divide the dough into 2 equal balls and wrap separately in plastic wrap. Place in the fridge for at least 1 hour or up to 3 days. The dough will keep in the freezer for up to 1 month. If using frozen dough, let it thaw in the fridge overnight or for about 1 hour at room temperature. The dough should be cold when you cut out the cookies.

Preheat the oven to 350°F (180°C).

Place a piece of parchment paper that is the same size as a baking sheet on your counter and place a ball of the dough on the parchment. Place a second piece of parchment over the dough. Roll out the dough ¼ inch (6 mm) thick. Peel off the top parchment and use 1 or more cookie cutters to cut out shapes, spacing them 1 inch (2.5 cm) apart. Alternatively, use an overturned glass to cut out rounds. Keep the cookies on the parchment and pull away the excess dough. Shape the excess dough into a ball, place between parchment sheets, roll out ¼ inch (6 mm) thick, and cut out more cookies.

Transfer the parchment paper with the cookies to a baking sheet. In a small bowl, beat the remaining 1 egg, then brush the cookies with it.

Bake the cookies until golden, 10–15 minutes. Let cool on the baking sheet for 15 minutes, then transfer to a wire rack to cool completely. While the first pan of cookies is baking, repeat with the second ball of dough to make more cookies. Bake a third batch of cookies from any excess dough scraps. The cookies will keep in an airtight container at room temperature for up to 2 weeks.

Makes about 40 cookies

butter
and
brunch

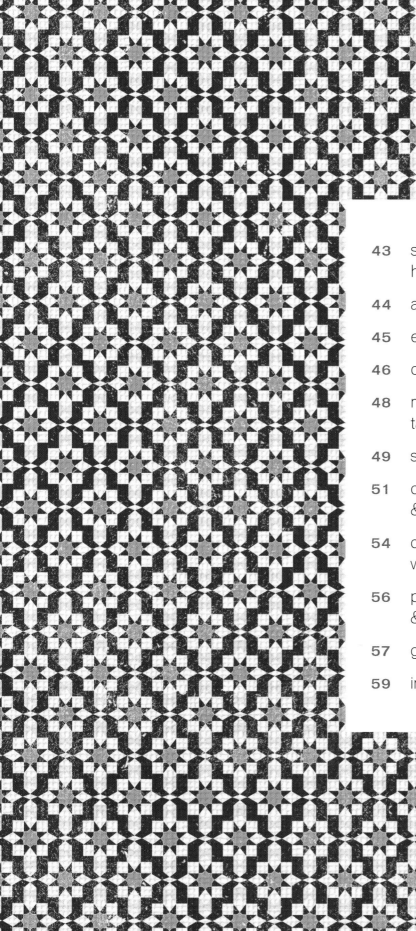

spinach & feta quiche with heirloom tomatoes

The flaky, buttery crust for this quiche is easy to make. The same dough can be used for the Peach & Raspberry Whole-Wheat Crostata on page 190. I often prepare a few batches of this versatile dough ahead of time and store it in the freezer until I need it, which makes throwing this recipe together super easy. The gorgeous heirloom tomato slices add a burst of color that will brighten your brunch buffet.

For the Crust

1	cup (5 oz/155 g) all-purpose flour
½	cup (2½ oz/75 g) whole-wheat flour
1½	teaspoons sugar
	Kosher salt
¾	cup (6 oz/185 g) cold unsalted butter, cubed
1	large egg, beaten
1	tablespoon whole milk or soy milk

For the Filling

5	large eggs, beaten
2	tablespoons whole milk
1½	cups (8 oz/250 g) frozen chopped spinach, thawed and squeezed of excess liquid
1	cup (5 oz/155 g) crumbled feta cheese
1	teaspoon onion powder
¼	teaspoon dried basil
	Kosher salt and freshly ground pepper
6-8	thin slices heirloom tomato

To make the crust, in a food processor, combine the flours, sugar, and ½ teaspoon salt and process for 5 seconds. Add the butter and pulse until the butter is reduced to small pieces. Add the egg and milk and pulse until moist clumps form.

Transfer the dough to a work surface, gather into a ball, and flatten into a disk. Wrap in plastic wrap and refrigerate for at least 1½ hours or up to 2 days. The dough will keep in the freezer for up to 3 months. If using frozen dough, let it thaw in the refrigerator overnight or at room temperature for about 1 hour.

Preheat the oven to 375°F (190°C).

On a piece of parchment paper, roll out the dough into a 12-inch (30-cm) round. Gently transfer to a 9-inch (23-cm) pie pan, fold the overhang under, and crimp or flute the edges. (It doesn't need to look perfect, as it will taste perfect!) Use a fork to pierce a few holes in the center of the dough. Bake until light brown, about 20 minutes. Transfer to a wire rack and let cool. Do not turn off the oven.

To make the filling, in a large bowl, whisk together the eggs, milk, spinach, cheese, onion powder, basil, a dash of salt, and ¼ teaspoon pepper. Pour the filling into the pie shell. Arrange the tomato slices on top.

Bake until the filling is set and the crust is golden brown, 30–40 minutes. Allow the quiche to cool slightly before serving. To make in advance, let cool, then cover with plastic wrap and freeze for up to 1 month. Thaw in the fridge overnight and reheat in a 350°F (180°C) oven until warm before serving.

Makes one 9-inch (23-cm) quiche; serves 6–8

asparagus & goat cheese quiche

If you're short on time and want to put something hearty and delicious on your table, this is the recipe for you. Frozen pie shells are sold in most supermarkets, though I regularly opt for a whole-wheat shell, which is more easily found in health-food stores. I buy a few at a time and store them in the freezer, so I always have them on hand. The asparagus in this recipe can be swapped out for other quick-cooking vegetables, such as chopped spinach or roasted peppers or sliced mushrooms or zucchini. Even better, use leftover roasted or grilled vegetables instead. Treat this simple quiche recipe as a base for your favorite flavors to create your own version. You'll find yourself turning to it time and time again. Everyone loves a good quiche.

1	store-bought frozen 9-inch (23-cm) pie shell
1	cup (4 oz/125 g) chopped asparagus or your vegetables of choice
5	large eggs, beaten
2	tablespoons whole milk
¼	lb (125 g) fresh goat cheese, crumbled, or ¾ cup (6 oz/185 g) ricotta cheese
1	teaspoon dried basil
1	teaspoon steak seasoning
	Kosher salt and freshly ground pepper
½	cup (2 oz/60 g) shredded cheese of choice, such as Cheddar, Parmesan, or Gruyère (optional)

Preheat the oven to 425°F (220°C).

Thaw the pie shell on the counter for 5 minutes. (Keep the shell in its original pan, but place the pan on a baking sheet in case of any leaks while baking.) Use a fork to pierce a few holes in the center of the pie shell. Bake until light brown, about 8 minutes.

Meanwhile, reserve about 8 pieces of asparagus for garnish. In a large bowl, whisk together the eggs and milk. Stir in the remaining asparagus, the goat cheese, basil, steak seasoning, ½ teaspoon salt, and ¼ teaspoon pepper.

Remove the pie shell from the oven and pour in the filling. Bake for about 20 minutes. Carefully remove the quiche from the oven. Sprinkle the shredded cheese, if using, over the top and garnish decoratively with the reserved asparagus. Bake until the center is firm, about 10 minutes longer. Allow the quiche to cool slightly before serving. To make in advance, let cool, then cover with plastic wrap and freeze for up to 1 month. Thaw in the fridge overnight and reheat in a 350°F (180°C) oven until warm before serving.

Makes one 9-inch (23-cm) quiche; serves 6–8

easy vanilla bean french toast

This recipe has become a Sunday morning staple in my household. I use my leftover homemade challah and just three additional ingredients to whip up this crazy-good French toast. Keep a jar of Vanilla Bean Sugar on hand in your pantry, and breakfast will be on the table in under five minutes!

P.S. All my friends request this French toast when they are coming over for brunch, and I've devised a great way to keep a big batch hot for serving. Instead of stacking the slices on a plate the traditional way, I overlap them slightly in a baking dish and keep them in a 200°F (95°C) oven until ready to serve.

4	large eggs, beaten
¼	cup (2 fl oz/60 ml) whole milk
1	tablespoon Vanilla Bean Sugar (page 37), plus more for sprinkling
	Unsalted butter for cooking
10	slices challah, homemade (page 30) or store-bought, each about ½ inch (12 mm) thick

In a shallow baking dish, whisk together the eggs, milk, and vanilla bean sugar.

In a large frying pan, melt 1 teaspoon butter over medium-high heat. Dip the challah slices, one at a time, into the egg mixture until completely coated. Fry 2 slices at a time, turning once, until lightly golden, about 2 minutes per side; don't press down on the slices as they cook. Repeat to cook the remaining challah, melting 1 teaspoon butter in the pan before cooking each batch.

Let the French toast cool for a few seconds, then sprinkle generously with vanilla bean sugar.

Serves 4–6

coconut-banana muffins

Coconut and dark chocolate are one of my favorite combinations. Here, I use this delightful combo to take an old favorite, the banana muffin, and turn it into what it was born to be! What I love most about adding the coconut is that it provides such a great flavor but is not fully identifiable as coconut. People always ask, "What's in that? Caramel? Roasted nuts?" There's another mystery ingredient that I add to the batter: vanilla yogurt. It lends creaminess, moisture, and simple deliciousness. These muffins are melt-in-your-mouth rich yet light, simple yet extraordinary. Kids go crazy for them, and no one else can resist them, either. Note that this recipe yields a large number of muffins, so you'll have plenty to store in the freezer until you need them. Just thaw the muffins at room temperature for a couple of hours when ready to use.

	Nonstick cooking spray for pan
3	large eggs
1¼	cups (10 oz/315 g) sugar
1¼	cups (10 fl oz/310 ml) rice bran oil or canola oil
2	teaspoons vanilla extract
3	cups (15 oz/465 g) all-purpose flour
1	teaspoon baking soda
	Kosher salt
3	ripe, brown bananas, peeled and cut into chunks
½	cup (2 oz/60 g) unsweetened shredded coconut
½	cup (4 oz/125 g) vanilla yogurt (Greek or regular)
1	cup (5 oz/150 g) chopped chocolate or mini chocolate chips (dark or semisweet)

Preheat the oven to 350°F (180°C). Spray two 12-cup standard muffin pans or two 24-cup mini muffin pans with nonstick cooking spray. If you decide to use paper liners, it is a good idea to spray them, as well.

In a stand mixer fitted with the paddle attachment, beat together the eggs, sugar, oil, and vanilla on high speed until well combined, about 2 minutes. Reduce the speed to low, add the flour, baking soda, and ½ teaspoon salt and beat until combined, about 2 minutes. Raise the speed to medium, add the bananas, coconut, and yogurt, and beat for 1 minute. Reduce the speed to low, add in the chocolate, and mix until well combined.

Using a small ice-cream scoop or measuring cup (for standard muffins) or a mini ice-cream scoop or very small measuring cup (for mini muffins), fill the prepared muffin cups almost to the top with batter.

Bake until a toothpick inserted into the center of a muffin comes out clean, 20–25 minutes for standard muffins or 15–20 minutes for mini muffins. Turn the muffins out onto a wire rack and let cool for at least 10 minutes before serving. The muffins will keep in an airtight container at room temperature for up to 1 week or in lock-top plastic freezer bags in the freezer for up to 1 month.

Makes 24 standard muffins or 48 mini muffins

mini pumpkin pie muffins with tart lemon glaze

These bite-sized muffins are great because they're tasty, easy to prepare, and loved by all. For Thanksgiving dinner, you can serve them for dessert or even as a side dish. I make a ton of them, wrap them in cellophane bags, and give them away to family and friends. The ultra-lemony glaze is really what takes these little treats to the next level. The combination of tart and sweet on a soft, crumbly, adorable mini muffin, plus the flavors of cinnamon and nutmeg, screams "autumn."

	Oil or butter for greasing pans
2	cups (10 oz/315 g) all-purpose flour
1	cup (8 oz/250 g) sugar
1	cup (8½ oz/265 g) pumpkin purée (fresh or canned)
3	large eggs plus 1 large egg white
1	teaspoon vanilla extract
2	teaspoons baking powder
2	teaspoons baking soda
1	teaspoon ground cinnamon
	Pinch of ground nutmeg
	Kosher salt

For the Tart Lemon Glaze

1	cup (4 oz/125 g) confectioners' sugar
	Grated zest and juice of 1½ lemons

Preheat the oven to 350°F (180°C). Grease two 12-cup mini muffin pans and line with paper liners. (If you have only 1 mini muffin pan, once you remove the baked muffins from it, let the pan cool, then grease it, line the cups with paper liners, and fill them with the remaining batter.) Alternatively, grease and line one 12-cup standard muffin pan.

In a large bowl, whisk together the flour, sugar, pumpkin purée, eggs and egg white, vanilla, baking powder, baking soda, cinnamon, nutmeg, and ½ teaspoon salt until smooth.

Using a mini ice-cream scoop or very small measuring cup for mini muffins or a small ice-cream scoop or small measuring cup for standard muffins, fill the prepared muffin cups almost to the top with the batter.

Bake until the muffins are golden and a toothpick inserted into the center comes out clean, about 20 minutes for 24 mini muffins or 30 minutes for 12 standard-sized muffins. Turn the muffins out onto a wire rack and let cool completely.

Meanwhile, make the glaze: In a small bowl, stir together the confectioners' sugar and lemon zest and juice until smooth. When the muffins are cool, use a spoon to drizzle the glaze over them. The muffins will keep in an airtight container at room temperature for up to 1 week or in lock-top plastic freezer bags in the freezer for up to 1 month. Thaw at room temperature for about 2 hours when ready to use.

Makes 24 mini muffins or 12 standard muffins

sticky date & caramel bread pudding

I love serving something indulgent at brunch—something that I can make with rich ingredients like butter and cream but that isn't overly sweet. This bread pudding has become my go-to recipe. The bits of dates literally melt into the caramel sauce, creating sticky, gooey goodness. Every single person to whom I have fed this goes crazy over it. Plus, you can make it ahead of time and freeze it. Who doesn't love that?

1	cup (6½ oz/200 g) pitted soft dates
½	teaspoon baking soda
1	teaspoon vanilla extract
1	large challah, homemade (page 30) or store-bought, cut into small cubes or thin slices
5	large eggs
4	tablespoons (2 oz/60 g) unsalted butter, melted and cooled
¼	cup (2 fl oz/60 ml) heavy cream or half-and-half
	Kosher salt

For the Caramel

½	cup (4 fl oz/125 ml) heavy cream
4	tablespoons (2 oz/60 g) unsalted butter
½	cup (3½ oz/105 g) firmly packed light or dark brown sugar

Preheat the oven to 350°F (180°C).

In a small saucepan, bring 1 cup (8 fl oz/250 ml) water to a boil over high heat. Add the dates and baking soda, reduce the heat to medium, and cook, stirring occasionally, until the mixture is bubbly and the dates have completely softened, about 10 minutes. Transfer the mixture to a heatproof bowl and stir in the vanilla. Using a handheld electric mixer, beat on high speed until creamy, about 3 minutes. Alternatively, transfer to a blender and process until creamy. Let cool.

Place the challah in a 15-by-10-inch (38-by-25-cm) glass baking dish. You can arrange the cubes or slices in neat layers or just throw them all in.

In a large bowl, whisk together the eggs, butter, cream, and a pinch of salt until foamy, about 2 minutes. Pour in the cooled date mixture and stir to combine. Pour evenly over the challah. Use your hands to push the challah down into the liquid to ensure all of the pieces are immersed. Cover the dish with aluminum foil and bake the pudding until it is golden and the edges are crisped, about 45 minutes.

Meanwhile, make the caramel: In a small saucepan, combine the cream, butter, and brown sugar. Place over medium heat and cook, stirring constantly, until a thick caramel forms, about 10 minutes. Be careful not to burn the caramel, or yourself! Keep the caramel on the lowest heat setting while the bread pudding bakes.

When the pudding is ready, remove it from the oven and let it cool for 5 minutes, then drizzle the caramel over the top. To make in advance, let cool completely, then cover with plastic wrap and freeze for up to 1 month. Thaw in the fridge overnight and reheat in a 350°F (180°C) oven until warm before serving.

Serves 8–10

dark chocolate, coconut & olive oil granola

If you love granola, you will really love granola when you make it at home. It is that much better. It's fresh and crunchy right out of the oven, and you can personalize it by choosing what goes into it. I know I say this about many recipes, but granola is surprisingly easy to make. You can also save money by preparing it yourself. Enjoy it with yogurt, strewn over ice cream, or on its own. Plus, granola is a great homemade gift idea.

3	cups (9 oz/280 g) rolled oats
¾	cup (3 oz/90 g) unsweetened shredded coconut
1	cup (4 oz/125 g) unsalted pumpkin seeds
1	cup (4 oz/125 g) unsalted sunflower seeds
1	cup (5 oz/155 g) chopped unsalted nuts (almonds, walnuts, or pecans)
½	teaspoon vanilla powder or extract
¾	cup (9 oz/280 g) raw honey or pure maple syrup
1	tablespoon melted coconut oil
½	cup (4 fl oz/125 ml) extra-virgin olive oil
	Kosher salt
1	bar (3 oz/90 g) dark chocolate (60% cacao or more)

Preheat the oven to 350°F (180°C).

On a large baking sheet, combine the oats, coconut, seeds, and nuts and mix well. Add the vanilla, honey, oils, and 1 teaspoon salt. Use your hands to mix all the ingredients together until the oats are evenly coated. Then use your hands to flatten the mixture in an even layer on the pan.

Bake for 10 minutes. Remove from the oven and use a spatula to move the granola around the baking sheet, pushing the granola on the edges into the center and vice versa. Reduce the oven temperature to 325°F (165°C) and bake for 10 minutes longer. Remove the pan from the oven again, move the granola around the pan as before, and return the pan to the oven. Bake for 10 minutes longer until the granola is golden and crisp, about 30 minutes total. The oats should be toasty and brown, but be careful not to burn them! Remove from the oven and let cool completely, about 10 minutes.

Use a sharp chef's knife to cut the chocolate bar crosswise into thin slivers, then chop the slivers crosswise, forming thin chunks. Add the chocolate to the cooled granola and toss to mix well. The granola will keep in a tightly capped glass jar at room temperature for up to 1 month.

Makes 4–5 cups (24–30 oz/750–940 g)

caramelized red onion & dill frittata with smoked salmon

Some of my favorite flavors come together in this recipe to create the ultimate frittata. Instead of cooking it in a frying pan, I use a springform pan, which allows for foolproof transferring to a serving dish. I always switch between using za'atar and chipotle chile powder to flavor this frittata (usually depends on who is eating it!). So here, I'm letting you choose between them.

1	tablespoon extra-virgin olive oil
1	red onion, thinly sliced
1	bunch fresh dill, finely chopped
8	slices smoked salmon, about ¼ lb (115 g) total weight, roughly chopped
1	tablespoon unsalted butter
8	large eggs, lightly beaten
1	tablespoon za'atar (for mild flavor) or chipotle chile powder (for some bite)
	Kosher salt and freshly ground pepper

Preheat the oven to 425°F (220°C).

In a large sauté pan, heat the oil over medium-high heat. Add the onion and cook, stirring occasionally, until caramelized and slightly crisped, 8–10 minutes. Remove from the heat and stir in the dill and salmon. Let stand for 5 minutes.

Meanwhile, put the butter in the base of a 10-inch (25-cm) springform pan. Place the pan in the oven until the butter melts, about 3 minutes. While the butter is melting, add the eggs, za'atar or chile powder, 1 teaspoon salt, and ½ teaspoon pepper to the onion mixture and whisk well.

Carefully remove the hot pan from the oven, swirl the melted butter around so it covers the base of the pan evenly, and pour in the egg mixture. Immediately return the pan to the oven and bake until the frittata is firm, about 25 minutes. Let cool for 5 minutes, then release the sides of the springform pan and transfer the frittata to a serving dish. Slice and serve warm or at room temperature.

Makes one 10-inch (25-cm) frittata; serves 6–8

penne with lemon zest, pine nuts & parmesan "pesto"

Whenever I am lucky enough to travel to Italy, I always find myself amazed at the delectable simplicity of the food. With each luscious bite I take, I can't help but announce every ingredient I taste in the dish. And that is why I love Italian food so much. You know what you are eating. The flavors are never masked. Instead, they highlight one another, which is what good food is all about. This is a simple pasta dish inspired by the many I've been fortunate enough to eat along the way. It's also one of my family's favorite dishes. This recipe is best made just before serving: the warm pasta and nuts melt the cheese, and everything combines in a lovely, silky way.

1	package (1 lb/500 g) penne pasta
1	cup (5 oz/155 g) pine nuts
	Finely grated zest of 2 lemons
2	cups (8 oz/250 g) grated Parmesan cheese
	Kosher salt and freshly ground pepper
4–5	tablespoons extra-virgin olive oil
1	cup (1 oz/30 g) fresh basil leaves, torn into small pieces

Bring a large pot of salted water to a boil over high heat. Add the pasta, stir well, and cook according to the package directions.

A few minutes before the pasta is ready, put the pine nuts in a small frying pan, place over medium-high heat, and stir continuously with a wooden spoon until the nuts are slightly golden, 3 minutes maximum. Be careful they do not burn. Transfer the nuts to a bowl and use the spoon to mash them a little, which releases their oils.

When the pasta is ready, drain and transfer it to a large serving bowl. Add the pine nuts, lemon zest, and cheese and toss well. Season with salt and pepper. Drizzle the oil over the pasta, add the basil, and toss to mix evenly. Serve right away.

Serves 4–6

giant ricotta ravioli with cinnamon

Before you read further, please let me assure you that this method of making ravioli is easy. You can do this! And you will blow away your guests. I mean, who makes ravioli? Now, you do. Instead of preparing the dough from scratch (really, who does that?), I use store-bought wonton wrappers. Dollop the center of each wrapper with the most mouthwatering, luscious lemon-ricotta filling and then cover with an additional wrapper, pressing down on the edges to create "ravioli." Once you master this recipe, you will make it often.

For the Ravioli

1⅓	cups (11 oz/345 g) ricotta cheese
	Zest of 1 lemon
2	teaspoons sugar
½	teaspoon ground cinnamon
	Kosher salt and freshly ground pepper
40	wonton wrappers
1	large egg, beaten

For the Lemon-Wine Sauce

3	tablespoons unsalted butter
½	cup (4 fl oz/125 ml) dry white wine
	Juice of 1 lemon
	Kosher salt
	Leaves from 2 fresh thyme sprigs

To make the ravioli, in a bowl, combine the cheese, lemon zest, sugar, cinnamon, and ¼ teaspoon each salt and pepper and mix well. Taste and adjust the seasoning. Set the filling aside.

Line a baking sheet with parchment paper. Lay 20 wonton wrappers on the prepared baking sheet. Brush a little bit of the egg wash over each wrapper, then place 1 tablespoon filling in the center of each wrapper. Cover with a second wonton wrapper and use your fingertips to press down firmly along the edges to seal well. You will have 20 filled ravioli. They can be tightly covered with plastic wrap and refrigerated for up to 12 hours before continuing.

Have a warmed serving platter handy. Bring a large pot of salted water to a boil over high heat. Reduce the heat so the water simmers and quickly drop in 5 ravioli, one at a time, and stir gently to separate them as they hit the water. Poach gently until the ravioli puff up slightly and float to the surface, 2–3 minutes. Using a slotted spoon, transfer the ravioli to the serving platter in a single layer, then cook the remaining ravioli the same way. Keep warm.

When you have finished cooking the ravioli, make the sauce: In a small sauté pan, melt the butter over medium-high heat. Add the wine, lemon juice, a pinch of salt, and the thyme, stir to combine, and cook for about 3 minutes to reduce slightly and blend the flavors. Spoon the sauce over the ravioli and serve right away.

Serves 6

individual mac & cheese

I love this recipe, adapted from *The Fannie Farmer Cookbook*, because it's simple and classic. But if you want to dress it up, it's easy to do. I add many things to my version to vary it: pesto, red pepper flakes, truffle oil, and toasted sesame oil, to name a few. Also, let's face it, macaroni and cheese is no longer just for kids. The dish has become the "it" food all over town. For a dinner party, I love pairing it with a main course of fish. My friends always rave. I guess it's one of those dishes that just puts you in a good mood. I prepare it in individual baking dishes or ramekins, so each guest gets his or her own bubbly and crisp serving right out of the oven. And FYI, you can make it in advance and freeze it.

Preheat the oven to 400°F (200°C). Butter eight ½-cup (4–fl oz/125-ml) ramekins or a 9-by-12-inch (23-by-30-cm) baking dish.

Bring a pot of salted water to a boil over high heat. Add the macaroni, stir well, and cook for a few minutes less than the package directions. Drain and set aside.

In a large saucepan, melt the butter over medium heat. Add the flour, ½ teaspoon salt, and a sprinkle of black pepper and whisk to stir until well blended. Gradually pour in the milk and cream while stirring constantly. Bring to a boil and boil, stirring, for 2 minutes. Reduce the heat to medium and cook, stirring, until the sauce thickens, about 10 minutes longer. Add the cheese little by little and simmer, stirring, until melted, about 5 minutes. Remove from the heat.

Transfer the macaroni to a large bowl, pour in the cheese sauce, and toss to coat evenly. Transfer to the prepared baking dishes and sprinkle with the cornflake crumbs. Bake until the top is golden brown, about 20 minutes for individual ramekins and 35 minutes for the baking dish. Just before serving, sprinkle with the pepper flakes or other topping.

To make in advance, let cool completely, then cover with plastic wrap and freeze for up to 1 month. Thaw in the fridge overnight and reheat in a preheated 325°F (165°C) oven for 20–25 minutes before serving.

Serves 8

4	tablespoons (2 oz/60 g) unsalted butter, plus butter for greasing dishes
1	package (8 oz/250 g) macaroni or other small pasta
¼	cup (1½ oz/45 g) all-purpose flour
	Kosher salt and freshly ground black pepper
1	cup (8 fl oz/250 ml) whole milk
1	cup (8 fl oz/250 ml) heavy cream
2	cups (8 oz/250 g) shredded Cheddar cheese or shredded cheese of your choice
½	cup (2 oz/60 g) cornflake crumbs
	Red pepper flakes, truffle oil, pesto, or toasted sesame oil for topping

soups
and
dips

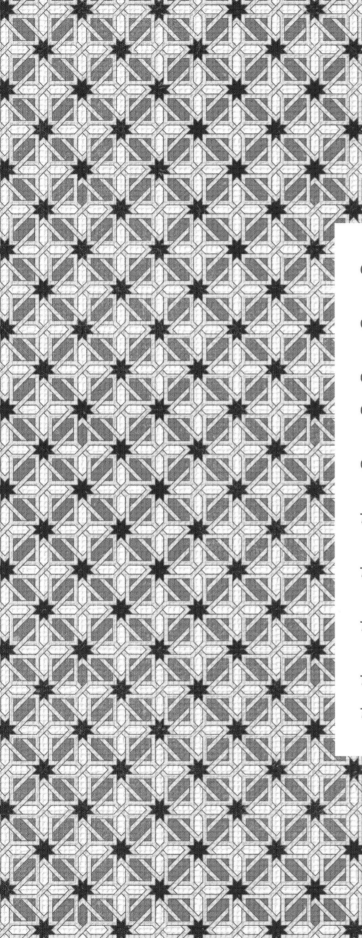

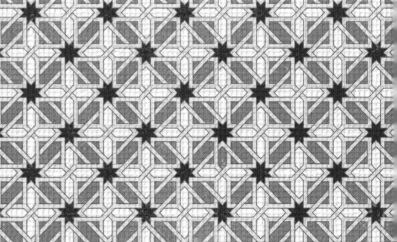

caramelized onion, fennel & mushroom soup

If you're looking for a soup recipe that is modern and unique, look no further. The sweet caramelized onions and fennel contrast with the earthy mushrooms, and together they create a sophisticated soup that is the ideal starter for a dinner party.

5	tablespoons (3 fl oz/80 ml) olive oil
6	yellow onions, about 1½ lb (750 g) total weight, thinly sliced
1	fennel bulb, trimmed, cored, and thinly sliced
1	clove garlic, minced
8	cups (64 fl oz/2 l) chicken, beef, or vegetable stock, warmed
1	lb (500 g) wild mushrooms, such as cremini, stemmed shiitake, and/or portobello, thinly sliced
¼	cup (2 fl oz/60 ml) dry white wine
	Kosher salt and freshly ground pepper
	Fresh basil leaves, torn into small pieces, for garnish

In a very large sauté pan, heat 4 tablespoons (2 fl oz/60 ml) of the oil over medium-high heat. Add the onions and cook, stirring occasionally, for 1–2 minutes. Reduce the heat to medium and cook, stirring occasionally, for 10 minutes longer.

Add the fennel to the onions and stir to combine. Continue cooking over medium heat until the vegetables are translucent and caramel colored, about 10 minutes. Add the garlic and cook for 1 minute longer. Transfer the onion mixture to a large pot and add the stock. Set aside.

In the same sauté pan (no need to clean it), heat the remaining 1 tablespoon oil over high heat. Add the mushrooms and cook, stirring occasionally, until softened, about 3 minutes. Add the wine, reduce the heat to low, and simmer until slightly reduced, about 5 minutes.

Add the mushroom mixture to the pot with the onion mixture and stir to combine. Bring the soup to a simmer over medium heat and season with salt and pepper. Ladle the soup into warmed bowls, garnish with basil, and serve right away.

To freeze the soup, divide into several small containers for smaller portions or transfer to 1 large container and freeze for up to 6 weeks. To serve, thaw in the fridge overnight, then transfer to a pot, place over medium heat, and heat until hot.

Serves 6–8

one-pot chicken soup with seasonal vegetables

My mother-in-law, Lee, introduced me to this wonderful recipe, and now I make this soup every time I come home from a long trip. I put everything into one pot, let it cook slowly on the stove top, and enjoy the delightful aroma until the soup is done. There is no easier or more delicious way to eat. Use vegetables that are in season. Here, I included Garnet yams (aka sweet potatoes), fennel, onions, and chicken drumsticks. (Be sure to give the fennel a try; it lends a mysterious, rich flavor.) I also added a splash of wine, a big bunch of fresh dill, and lots of salt and pepper. But these just happened to be the ingredients I had on hand. Make this recipe your own. Use any chicken parts you prefer, or even a whole bird. Add zucchini, tomatoes, spinach, or mushrooms to make the soup as heavy or as light as you wish. If you love garlic, throw some into the pot. If you don't have fresh herbs, use dried ones. You can't go wrong. This soup freezes well, too.

6	skin-on, bone-in chicken drumsticks or other pieces of your choice, about 1½ lb (750 g)
2	yellow onions, cut into chunks
1	large Garnet yam, peeled and cut into chunks
1	fennel bulb, trimmed, cored, and cut into chunks
1	bunch fresh dill, roughly chopped
	Splash of white wine (optional)
	Kosher salt and freshly ground pepper

In a large pot, combine the chicken, onions, yam, fennel, dill, and wine, and season with salt and pepper. Add enough cold water to cover. Place over high heat and bring to a simmer, then reduce the heat to medium-low. Cover and cook until the vegetables break up easily with a fork, 1½–2 hours.

Remove the chicken from the pot. When cool enough to handle, remove the meat from the bones, discarding the skin and bones, and cut the meat into bite-sized pieces. Return the meat to the pot. If you'd like the soup a little thicker, place the pot over high heat, bring to a simmer, and cook, uncovered, until thickened to your liking, 10–15 minutes. Taste and season as necessary.

To freeze the soup, divide into several small containers for smaller portions or transfer to 1 large container and freeze for up to 6 weeks. To serve, thaw in the fridge overnight, then transfer to a pot, place over medium heat, and heat until hot.

Serves 8–10

butternut squash & corn chowder

Creamy but chunky, this soup combines roasted butternut squash, lots of golden onions, and crunchy corn kernels. It comes together in three quick steps and freezes well. Keep the corn kernels frozen until you're ready to add them to the soup.

3	large yellow onions, diced
1	large butternut squash, about 2 lb (1 kg), peeled, halved, seeded, and cubed
4	fresh thyme sprigs
¼	cup (2 fl oz/60 ml) olive oil
1–2	cups (8–16 fl oz/250–500 ml) vegetable or chicken stock or water, warmed
1½	cups (9 oz/280 g) frozen corn kernels
	Kosher salt and freshly ground pepper

Preheat the oven to 375°F (190°C). Line a baking sheet with parchment paper.

Place the onions, butternut squash, and thyme on the prepared baking sheet. Drizzle them with the oil, use your hands to toss together, and then spread in an even layer. Cover with aluminum foil and place in the oven for 30 minutes. Remove the foil and roast until the onions are golden and the squash is soft, about 30 minutes longer. Let cool for 10 minutes. Discard the thyme sprigs.

Transfer the onions and squash to a large food processor. If your processor isn't big enough to hold all the vegetables, work in batches. Be sure to scrape up all the little bits on the parchment and add them to the processor. Pulse until creamy.

Transfer the puréed vegetables to a pot and add enough stock until the soup is the desired consistency. I like it medium-thick. Place over medium heat and heat until piping hot. Stir in the frozen corn and season with salt and pepper. Ladle into warmed bowls and serve right away.

To freeze the soup, divide into several small containers for smaller portions or transfer to 1 large container and freeze for up to 6 weeks. To serve, thaw in the fridge overnight, then transfer to a pot, place over medium heat, and heat until hot.

Serves 6–8

yam & chickpea purée with crispy sage

This combination is surprisingly tasty and healthy. The buttery burnt sage leaves add the perfect amount of creaminess. I love serving a bowl of this silky soup before a main course of fish.

5	large Garnet yams, about 2 lb (1 kg) total weight, peeled and cut into small cubes
2	tablespoons extra-virgin olive oil
4	tablespoons (2 oz/60 g) unsalted butter
1	can (15½ oz/485 g) chickpeas, drained and rinsed
2	cloves garlic, minced
6–8	fresh sage leaves
4	cups (32 fl oz/1 l) vegetable stock or water, warmed
	Kosher salt and freshly ground pepper

Preheat the oven to 375°F (190°C). Line a baking sheet with parchment paper.

Place the yams on the prepared baking sheet. Drizzle them with the oil, use your hands to toss together, then spread in an even layer. Cover with aluminum foil and bake until tender, about 30 minutes. Let cool for 10 minutes.

Meanwhile, in a large sauté pan, melt the butter over medium-low heat. Add the chickpeas, garlic, and sage leaves, reduce the heat to low, and cook, stirring occasionally, until the butter browns, the garlic is golden, and the sage leaves are crisp, about 10 minutes. Use tongs to pick out the sage leaves and reserve.

Transfer the yams to a large pot and add the chickpea mixture, scraping up all the bits from the sauté pan and adding them, as well. Add the stock and stir to combine. Use an immersion blender to purée into a creamy soup. Alternatively, working in batches, transfer the soup to a stand blender or a food processor and purée, then transfer it to a clean pot. Place over medium heat and heat until piping hot. Ladle into warmed bowls and garnish with the sage leaves, either whole or chopped into pieces.

To freeze the soup, divide into several small containers for smaller portions or transfer to 1 large container and freeze for up to 6 weeks. To serve, thaw in the fridge overnight, then transfer to a pot, place over medium heat, and heat until hot. (Heat fresh sage leaves in butter over low heat until crisp to use for garnish.)

Serves 6–8

lentil soup with carrots, lemon & greens

Some days all you want is a big bowl of soup. Here's an awesome recipe for one that is delicious, rich, and soul warming. It is Mediterranean inspired and calls for lentils, carrots, celery, and onions, though you can use other vegetables you have on hand. I added some lemon slices to the pot because I knew they would add a welcome zestiness. When the soup was done, I found some kale in my fridge, tore it into bite-sized pieces, and threw them into the pot. They delivered great color, texture, and taste. If you don't have kale, try spinach, Swiss chard, or any robust leafy green. You can make a huge pot of this soup and freeze some of it to have on hand the next time a craving hits. And even if you don't love curry, this soup is still for you. The curry taste is very mild, imparting only a deep, toasty flavor to the bowl.

2	tablespoons extra-virgin olive oil
2	yellow onions, diced
3	carrots, peeled and diced
2	ribs celery, diced
2	cloves garlic, minced
2	teaspoons curry powder
1	cup (7 oz/220 g) brown or pink lentils, rinsed
1	can (15 oz/470 g) diced tomatoes with juice
8	cups (64 fl oz/2 l) water or vegetable or chicken stock
1	lemon, sliced
	Kosher salt and freshly ground pepper
1	tablespoon sweet paprika (optional)
2	handfuls of kale, spinach, or other greens, torn into small pieces

In a large pot, heat the oil over medium-high heat. Add the onions and cook, stirring occasionally, until translucent, about 5 minutes. Add the carrots, celery, and garlic and cook, stirring occasionally, for 5 minutes. Stir in the curry powder until well combined.

Add the lentils, tomatoes and juice, water, and lemon slices and bring the soup to a simmer. Reduce the heat to medium, cover partially, and cook until the lentils have opened up but are not mushy, about 35 minutes.

Remove from the heat and discard the lemon slices if desired. Season the soup generously with salt and pepper. Stir in the paprika, if using, and the kale and cover tightly just long enough to wilt the kale. Ladle into warmed bowls and serve right away.

To freeze the soup, divide into several small containers for smaller portions or transfer to 1 large container and freeze for up to 6 weeks. To serve, thaw in the fridge overnight, then transfer to a pot, place over medium heat, and heat until hot.

Serves 10–12

rustic tomato soup with grilled cheese croutons

I made this soup almost by accident on a cold winter day. I opened the fridge and stared at a variety of tomatoes: two large beefsteaks, some superripe tomatoes, a storage container filled with sliced tomatoes (leftovers from the bagel and lox platter I'd ordered the day before), and a box of colorful cherry tomatoes. I had to come up with something, and it was easier than I thought. I just threw every tomato I had, including oil-packed sun-dried tomatoes, into a large pot. I simmered them together and then puréed the soup. The result was spectacular. I was going to serve it with grilled cheese sandwiches, but at the last minute, I decided to cut them into bite-sized croutons, and that decision got me rave reviews. Note that the measurements in this recipe are not exact—a little more or a little less is fine.

2	tablespoons extra-virgin olive oil
2	carrots, peeled and diced
1	large white or yellow onion, diced
2	ribs celery, finely diced
1–2	cans (15 oz/470 g each) diced tomatoes with juice
1–3	fresh tomatoes (cut up large tomatoes and keep smaller ones whole)
½	cup (4 oz/125 g) oil-packed sun-dried tomatoes with oil (optional)
1	can (6 oz/185 g) tomato paste
1–2	cans (8 oz/250 g each) tomato sauce
	Leaves from 1 bunch basil
	Kosher salt and freshly ground black pepper
	Extra-virgin olive oil, chile oil, or red pepper flakes for garnish (optional)

In a large pot, heat the oil over medium-high heat. Add the carrots, onion, and celery, cover, and cook, stirring occasionally, for 5 minutes. Uncover, stir well, and cook, uncovered, until softened and translucent, about 5 minutes longer.

Add all the tomatoes and juice, tomato paste, and tomato sauce and stir gently. Bring to a simmer, then cover, reduce the heat to medium-low, and cook until everything is soft and "melting" together, 30–40 minutes.

Meanwhile, prepare the grilled cheese croutons (see opposite).

When the soup is ready, add the basil and then use an immersion blender to blend everything together into a smooth purée. Alternatively, working in batches, transfer the soup to a stand blender or a food processor and purée, then transfer it to a clean pot. Taste and season generously with salt and black pepper and heat until piping hot. Ladle into warmed bowls and drizzle with olive oil or chile oil, or sprinkle with red pepper flakes, if using. Top each serving with 5 or 6 croutons and serve right away.

To freeze the soup, divide into several small containers for smaller portions or transfer to 1 large container and freeze for up to 6 weeks. To serve, thaw in the fridge overnight, then transfer to a pot, place over medium heat, and heat until hot.

Serves 8–10

For the Grilled Cheese Croutons

2	cups (8 oz/250 g) shredded or crumbled cheese, such as mozzarella, Muenster, or goat cheese
8	bread slices (I use honey whole wheat)
	Lots of unsalted butter, at room temperature

Put one-fourth of the cheese on each of 4 of the bread slices, spreading it evenly. Top each cheese-covered slice with a second bread slice. Spread the outside of both sides of each sandwich with butter.

To cook the sandwiches with a panini press (if you don't own one, it's a great investment): Cook the sandwiches, two at a time, until golden and toasty, about 4 minutes. Transfer to a cutting board and let cool. Use a sharp knife to cut the sandwiches into tiny cubes.

To cook the sandwiches on the stove top: Heat a frying pan over medium-high heat. Place a sandwich in the pan and put a heavy plate on the sandwich to press it down as it cooks. Cook, turning once and replacing the plate, until golden and sizzling on both sides, about 2 minutes on each side. Transfer to a cutting board, let cool, and cut as directed above. Repeat with the remaining sandwiches.

The croutons will keep in an airtight container in the fridge for up to 3 days. When ready to serve, place them on a baking sheet and heat in a preheated 375°F (190°C) oven for 10 minutes to crisp them up and make them melty inside.

Makes 50–60 croutons

charred eggplant dip with maple drizzle

This is a smoky but sweet eggplant dip probably unlike any you've tasted before. If you have a gas stove, I recommend charring the eggplant directly on the open flame. An outdoor grill is also a good way to achieve the smoky flavor. But don't worry if you don't have either. You can roast the eggplant in a hot oven and you'll still get an extra kick of smokiness from the cumin. This dip is fantastic served with pita chips or crudités.

1	large eggplant
1	tablespoon tahini
1	1-inch (2.5-cm) piece fresh ginger, peeled and grated
	Juice of ½ lemon
½	teaspoon ground cumin
	Kosher salt and freshly ground pepper
2	tablespoons pure maple syrup
	Rose buds for garnish (optional)

To char the eggplant on a gas stove top: Turn on a burner to high heat. Place the eggplant directly on the open flame and cook, turning with tongs, until the eggplant is charred on the outside and completely softened on the inside, about 6 minutes per side. Place the eggplant in a plastic bag for 10 minutes, then carefully peel away the charred skin and discard. Place the flesh in a bowl, discarding any large seed pockets.

To char the eggplant on an outdoor grill: Prepare a hot fire in a charcoal or gas grill. Place the eggplant on the grill and cook, turning with tongs, until the eggplant is charred on the outside and completely softened on the inside, about 6 minutes per side. Place the eggplant in a plastic bag for 10 minutes, then peel as directed above.

To char the eggplant in the oven: Preheat the oven to 450°F (230°C). Wrap the eggplant in aluminum foil and place in a baking dish. Roast until the eggplant is completely softened on the inside, about 30 minutes. Let cool in the foil for about 20 minutes, then unwrap and peel as directed above.

Use a fork to mash the eggplant flesh. Whisk in the tahini, ginger, lemon juice, and cumin and season generously with salt and pepper. Transfer to a serving dish, drizzle with the maple syrup, and garnish with rose petals, if desired. This dip is best made just before serving but will keep in an airtight container in the fridge for up to 2 days.

Makes about 1 cup (6 oz/185 g)

ginger-scallion dip with sesame seeds

This isn't the usual type of dip. Instead, it is a small bowl of gold. Teeny pieces of ginger and scallions are slowly simmered until they reach a jamlike consistency. I am always looking for a spicy condiment to serve alongside roast chicken or grilled fish. Accompanying a simple main course with a dip like this one instantly transforms the dish from "everyday" to "gourmet." Because the flavors of the ginger and scallions are so intense, each diner needs just a small dollop of this dip. You may be surprised to find that the large number of scallions reduces to only a small amount once they've been sautéed. A Microplane grater makes fast work of grating the ginger.

15	scallions
2	tablespoons extra-virgin olive oil
1	3-inch (7.5-cm) piece fresh ginger, peeled and grated
3	tablespoons soy sauce
	Freshly ground pepper
2	tablespoons sesame seeds

Trim the root end off each scallion, and cut off and discard the dark green tops. Chop the scallions into tiny pieces.

In a large sauté pan, heat the oil over medium-high heat. Add the scallions and cook, stirring constantly, until softened, about 4 minutes. Add the ginger and cook, stirring constantly, for 1 minute. Stir in the soy sauce and a pinch of pepper, reduce the heat to low, and cook, stirring occasionally, until the soy sauce is reduced and the mixture has thickened, about 10 minutes. Remove from the heat and stir in the sesame seeds. Transfer to a serving bowl and serve warm or at room temperature.

If not using right away, transfer to a glass jar. The dip will keep in the fridge for up to 1 week.

Makes about 1 cup (5 oz/155 g)

white bean, garlic & rosemary dip

Here is a great, quick dip recipe that is perfect served with crudités, za'atar-dusted pita chips (page 17), and a glass of red wine. The sharp toasted garlic contrasts with the warm, woodsy flavors of the rosemary. In the wintertime, I like to serve this dip slightly warm. Just fill a large bowl with boiling water and place the sealed container of dip directly in it for about 5 minutes. Then carefully remove the container and transfer the dip to a serving dish.

2	teaspoons extra-virgin olive oil
2	cloves garlic, cut into thin slivers
1	teaspoon fresh rosemary leaves or ½ teaspoon dried rosemary
2	cans (15 oz/470 g each) cannellini beans, drained and rinsed
	Kosher salt and freshly ground pepper
	Raw pure honey for drizzling

In a large sauté pan, heat the oil over medium heat. Add the garlic and cook, stirring constantly, until golden, about 3 minutes. Stir in the rosemary and cook, stirring constantly, for 1 minute. Add the beans and toss to combine.

Transfer the bean mixture to a food processor and pulse until a paste forms, scraping down the sides of the work bowl as needed. Season generously with salt and pepper.

Transfer the dip to a serving dish and drizzle with a little honey before serving. The dip will keep in an airtight container in the fridge for up to 1 week.

Makes about 2 cups (14 oz/440 g)

red chimichurri sauce

I always keep a jar of homemade *chimichurri* sauce in my fridge. It's wonderful on grilled meats and fish, lending bright color and flavor. I also enjoy pairing a jar of this salsa-style sauce with a bottle of my favorite red wine as a hostess gift. Something about the combo of spicy *chimichurri* and red wine works perfectly in my mind! For a milder sauce, use the jalapeño chile; if you prefer a hotter version, go with the habanero.

2	tomatoes, chopped, or 1 cup (6 oz/185 g) cherry tomatoes
1	red bell pepper, seeded and roughly chopped
1	handful of fresh basil leaves
1	handful of fresh flat-leaf parsley leaves or other fresh herbs, such as dill, cilantro, oregano, or mint
2	cloves garlic
1	1-inch (2.5-cm) piece fresh ginger, peeled and roughly chopped
1	jalapeño chile or ½ small habanero chile, stemmed and then seeded if desired
	Kosher salt and freshly ground pepper
¼	cup (2 fl oz/60 ml) extra-virgin olive oil

In a food processor, combine the tomatoes and bell pepper and pulse just until chopped. Add the basil, parsley, garlic, ginger, and jalapeño and pulse until the ingredients are minced and combined. Season with salt and pepper, drizzle with the oil, and process for 10 seconds more.

If not using right away, transfer to a tightly capped glass jar. The chimichurri will keep in the fridge for up to 1 week.

Makes one 6-oz (185-ml) jar, or about 1 cup (6 oz/185 g)

more
than
salad

fresh corn, sugar snap pea & tomato salad

For this recipe, I boil ears of corn and then I cut the kernels off the cobs. It's also a great summer salad to make with leftover ears of corn. I used to keep the corncobs in the fridge for my babies to teethe on—they loved it! The ingredients for the dressing go directly into the salad, making for a fast cleanup. Serve this salad as a side dish with grilled fish or meats. People always go crazy for it because the mix of ingredients is unusual.

6	ears corn, husks and silk removed, boiled just until tender
2	cups (4 oz/125 g) sugar snap peas, trimmed and julienned
3	cups (18 oz/560 g) mixed cherry and grape tomatoes, halved
1	handful of roughly chopped fresh cilantro
1	handful of roughly chopped fresh mint
¼	cup (2 fl oz/60 ml) red wine vinegar
3	tablespoons extra-virgin olive oil
2	tablespoons sugar
1	tablespoon dried basil
	Kosher salt and freshly ground pepper

Use a sharp knife to cut the kernels off the cobs. In a large bowl, combine the corn, snap peas, tomatoes, cilantro, mint, vinegar, oil, sugar, and basil. Season with salt and pepper and toss to mix well.

This salad can be made up to 5 hours in advance. Cover and store in the fridge.

Serves 6–8

pomelo salad with red onion, mint & cilantro

Pomelos are a citrus fruit with a sweet, mild grapefruit taste. When I was a teenager, I would sit around my parents' kitchen table for hours peeling giant pomelos and eating them with my friends on Friday nights after Shabbat dinner (wild child, what can I say?). The fruit is rather large and takes some time to peel, so I suggest peeling the pomelos and chopping or breaking the segments into small pieces in advance. Then store the pieces in an airtight container in the refrigerator to have on hand for this salad or just for munching!

1	pomelo
1	cup (6 oz/185 g) cherry tomatoes, halved
½	red onion, very thinly sliced
2	cups (2 oz/60 g) mizuna or baby arugula
¼	cup (¼ oz/7 g) fresh mint leaves, roughly chopped
¼	cup (¼ oz/7 g) fresh cilantro leaves, roughly chopped
	Juice of 1 lime
¼	cup (2 fl oz/60 ml) extra-virgin olive oil
	Pinch of sugar
	Kosher salt and freshly ground pepper

Using a sharp knife, cut a slice off the top and bottom of the pomelo just thick enough to reveal the flesh. Stand the pomelo upright on the cutting board and, following the contour of the fruit, cut downward to remove the peel and pith in wide strips, rotating the fruit as you work. Then, holding the fruit in one hand, cut along each side of the membrane between the segments, freeing the segments from the membrane. Chop the segments into bite-sized pieces.

In a shallow bowl, toss together the pomelo, tomatoes, onion, mizuna, mint, and cilantro.

In a small bowl, whisk together the lime juice, oil, and sugar until blended. Whisk in ¼ teaspoon each salt and pepper.

Cover the salad and dressing and store in the fridge for at least 20 minutes or for up to 2 hours. (This salad is meant to be served cool.) Just before serving, spoon the dressing over the salad and use your hands to toss together.

Serves 4–6

artichoke, tomato & olive salad

The key to this salad is to use antipasto ingredients that you love. If you're crazy about spicy olives, throw in a bunch. If you like roasted peppers, add them. Make sure to incorporate the oils and sauces from jarred and bottled ingredients. Don't drain any of the vegetables; instead, scoop them out with their liquid.

½	cup (3 oz/90 g) marinated artichoke hearts, quartered
¼	cup (2 oz/60 g) oil-packed sun-dried tomatoes
¼	cup (1 ½ oz/45 g) marinated olives
2	heirloom tomatoes, thinly sliced
1	avocado, pitted, peeled, and thinly sliced
	Extra-virgin olive oil for drizzling
	Juice of ½ lemon
	Kosher salt and freshly ground black pepper
	Red pepper flakes for sprinkling
	Crusty baguette or Homemade Pita Chips with Za'atar (page 17) for serving

In a bowl, combine the artichoke hearts, sun-dried tomatoes, olives, heirloom tomatoes, and avocado. Drizzle with oil and lemon juice and season with salt, black pepper, and red pepper flakes. Stir gently until blended.

Let stand for about 15 minutes before serving to allow the flavors to mingle. Serve with a crusty baguette.

Serves 4

shredded romaine with seeds & sweet onion vinaigrette

When it comes to salad, I need "bite." Soggy just doesn't cut it for me. My friend Natali introduced me to the technique of shredding romaine lettuce the way I would shred cabbage to make coleslaw, and I never looked back! Throw in some curry-spiced seeds for a little extra crunch and heat, and you've got a perfect salad.

For the Sweet Onion Vinaigrette

¼	cup (2 fl oz/60 ml) balsamic vinegar
1	tablespoon whole-grain Dijon mustard
1	tablespoon raw pure honey or agave nectar
½	cup (4 fl oz/125 ml) extra-virgin olive oil
½	small red onion, minced
½	teaspoon dried basil
½	teaspoon dried thyme
	Kosher salt and freshly ground pepper
1	large beefsteak tomato
2–3	small heads romaine lettuce
3	ribs celery
½	cup (2 oz/60 g) Curry-Spiced Mixed Seeds (page 19)

To make the vinaigrette, in a small bowl, whisk together the vinegar, mustard, honey, and oil until well blended. Add the onion, basil, thyme, and a pinch each of salt and pepper and stir well. The vinaigrette will keep in a tightly capped jar in the fridge for up to 2 weeks.

Use a mandoline or a very sharp knife to cut the tomato into superthin slices. Arrange the slices in a single layer on a platter. Use the mandoline or knife to shred the lettuce and then sprinkle it evenly over the tomato. Cut the celery into very thin slices and sprinkle it over the lettuce. Sprinkle the seeds evenly over the top and drizzle the vinaigrette over the salad. There's no need to toss together; the vinaigrette should just seep into the salad.

Serves 6–8

kohlrabi, edamame & carrots in ginger-miso marinade

The ginger-miso marinade in this recipe is thick and so mind-blowingly delicious that you'll want to eat it by the spoonful. I usually double the marinade recipe and use it on many different salads, such as the Fresh Corn, Sugar Snap Pea & Tomato Salad on page 81 or a simple green salad. I like raw kohlrabi in salads for its great crunch, but if you aren't a fan, just leave it out or substitute jicama.

4	large carrots, about ½ lb (250 g) total weight, peeled and cut into matchsticks
3	kohlrabi bulbs, peeled and cut into matchsticks
1	cup (5 oz/155 g) frozen shelled edamame, thawed
2	handfuls of sugar snap peas, trimmed and sliced

For the Ginger-Miso Marinade

2	carrots, peeled and cut into chunks
1	2-inch (5-cm) piece fresh ginger, peeled and cut into chunks
½	cup (4 oz/125 g) white miso
¼	cup (2 fl oz/60 ml) canola oil
1	teaspoon toasted sesame oil
¼	cup (2 fl oz/60 ml) rice vinegar
1	tablespoon raw pure honey
2	tablespoons toasted sesame seeds

In a bowl, toss together the carrots, kohlrabi, edamame, and snap peas.

To make the marinade, in a food processor, combine the carrots and ginger and pulse until finely chopped. Add the miso, oils, vinegar, honey, and ¼ cup (2 fl oz/60 ml) water and process until thickened. Transfer to a glass jar and stir in the sesame seeds.

Pour about 1 cup (8 fl oz/250 ml) of the marinade over the salad and toss well. Store the remaining marinade in the tightly capped jar in the fridge for up to 1 month.

Serves 6–8

cucumber, pomegranate & corn salad with poppy seeds

This salad is a major crowd-pleaser and very easy to boot. It always amazes me how much both kids and adults like it. Serve over leftover room-temperature basmati rice for a one-dish lunch.

4	Kirby (pickling) cucumbers, about 1 lb (500 g) total weight, thinly sliced into rounds
1	cup (6 oz/185 g) cooked corn kernels (fresh or canned)
¼	cup (1½ oz/45 g) pomegranate seeds
1	tablespoon poppy seeds
3	tablespoons rice vinegar
1	tablespoon extra-virgin olive oil
¼	teaspoon toasted sesame oil
½	teaspoon sugar
	Kosher salt and freshly ground pepper

In a bowl, toss together the cucumbers, corn, pomegranate seeds, and poppy seeds.

In a small glass bowl, whisk together the vinegar, oils, and sugar until the sugar dissolves. Whisk in a pinch each of salt and pepper. Drizzle the dressing over the salad and toss to mix well. Serve right away.

Serves 4–6

kale, carrot & radish salad with balsamic splash

The two ingredients I have in my fridge at all times are carrots and radishes. That's pretty much how they found their way into this salad, and it has been a Sunday night staple in our home ever since. I use shredded kale, but you can substitute any shredded lettuce you like. Color, crunch, and a good dressing—everything I think a salad should have—are all here. If you have a mandoline, use it to slice the carrots and radishes as thinly as possible.

3	cups (7 oz/200 g) shredded kale or mesclun greens
2	large carrots, peeled and very thinly sliced lengthwise
4–6	radishes, very thinly sliced into rounds
2	tablespoons drained capers
¼	cup (2 fl oz/60 ml) balsamic vinegar
½	cup (4 fl oz/125 ml) extra-virgin olive oil
1	small clove garlic, minced
3	tablespoons pure maple syrup
½	teaspoon dried thyme
	Kosher salt and freshly ground pepper

In a large bowl, toss together the kale, carrots, radishes, and capers.

In a glass jar, combine the vinegar, oil, garlic, maple syrup, thyme, and a generous pinch each of salt and pepper and shake until well blended. The dressing will keep in the capped jar in the fridge for up to 2 weeks.

Spoon some of the dressing over the salad (you won't need all of it), toss to mix well, and serve right away.

Serves 6–8

savoy slaw with lemongrass & lime dressing

The beauty of this recipe is that both the salad and the dressing can be made in a food processor. Use the shredding blade to shred the cabbage, carrots, and beet—there's no need to clean the bowl after each vegetable—then switch to the metal blade and process all the dressing ingredients together.

For the Slaw

1	small head savoy cabbage, cut into chunks
2	carrots, peeled and cut into chunks
1	beet, peeled and cut into chunks
1	cup (2 oz/60 g) sugar snap peas, trimmed and julienned
¼	cup (1 oz/30 g) salted, roasted sunflower seeds

For the Dressing

	Juice of 3 limes
2	tablespoons rice vinegar
1	lemongrass stalk, white part only, cut into small pieces
1	small scallion, roughly chopped
1	heaping tablespoon melted coconut oil
¼	cup (2 fl oz/60 ml) olive oil
1	tablespoon coconut sugar or granulated sugar
	Kosher salt and freshly ground pepper

To make the slaw, in a food processor fitted with the shredding disk, finely shred the cabbage. Transfer to a large bowl. Shred the carrots and then beets in the processor and add to the bowl. Toss in the snap peas and sunflower seeds.

To make the dressing, fit the processor with the metal blade and add the lime juice, vinegar, lemongrass, scallion, oils, and sugar to the work bowl. Pulse until well blended. Season with ¼ teaspoon each salt and pepper.

Pour the dressing over the slaw and toss. Let stand for 10 minutes before serving to allow the flavors to mingle.

Serves 6–8

avocado, hearts of palm, edamame & za'atar salad

When I was growing up, every Friday night there was a salad made of avocado and hearts of palm on the Shabbat table. Sometimes my mom would add a can of corn to it. To this day, it's still the salad that all the grandkids fight over. In this version, I've omitted the usual mayo and seasoned it with za'atar, which is an ingredient the kids have come to love. I like to serve this salad on a platter, instead of in a bowl, so the avocado doesn't get mushy.

2	avocados, pitted, peeled, and thinly sliced
	Juice of ½ lemon
6–8	hearts of palm (from 1 can or jar), cut into thin rounds
1	cup (5 oz/155 g) frozen shelled edamame, thawed
2	tablespoons za'atar
2	tablespoons extra-virgin olive oil
1	tablespoon rice vinegar
1	teaspoon pure raw honey
	Kosher salt and freshly ground pepper
	Grated zest of 1 lemon

Place the avocado slices in a single layer on a platter and drizzle the lemon juice over the slices. Scatter the hearts of palm over the avocados and top with the edamame. Sprinkle the za'atar over the salad.

In a small bowl, whisk together the oil, vinegar, and honey until blended. Season with salt and pepper. Spoon the dressing over the salad and garnish with the lemon zest. Serve right away.

Serves 6–8

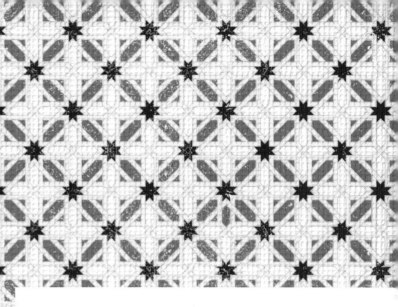

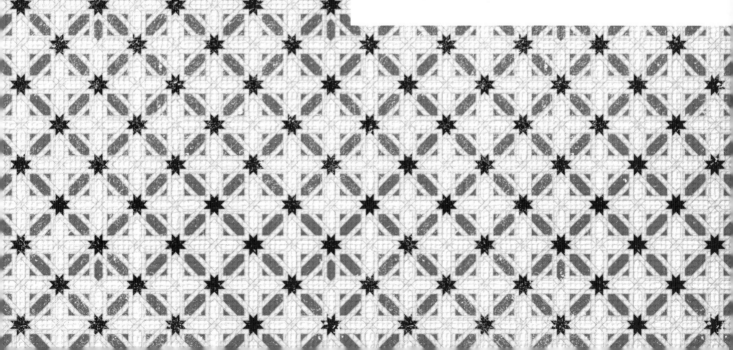

poisson à la marocaine

To me, nothing defines Moroccan cooking more than the classical preparation of fish. The vibrant red, yellow, and green colors, the spicy aroma, and the delicate textures all come together in this perfect dish. Traditionally, the fish is assembled and marinated in the fridge overnight, but if you are short on time, you can easily go ahead and cook it straightaway.

For the Paprika Oil

½	cup (1¾ oz/55 g) sweet paprika
2	cups (16 fl oz/500 ml) canola oil

For the Saffron Water

1	tablespoon saffron threads
1	cup (8 fl oz/250 ml) boiling water

4	cloves garlic, quartered
1	bunch fresh cilantro, stems reserved and left whole, leaves chopped
2	red bell peppers, seeded and finely diced
3	dried red chiles, such as guajillo, ancho, or pasilla
6	grouper or tilapia fillets, about 6 oz (185 g) each
1–2	preserved lemons, cut into small pieces
	Kosher salt and freshly ground pepper
	Fresh cilantro for garnish

To make the paprika oil, in a glass jar, combine the paprika and oil and shake until well blended. Set aside. This will serve as the base for your Moroccan cooking. Store in a dark pantry and always shake before using.

To make the saffron water, preheat the oven to 425°F (220°C). Place the saffron on a small piece of aluminum foil and fold over to secure the saffron inside. Toast in the oven for no more than 1 minute. Use your fingers to crumble the saffron into tiny pieces. Place in a small glass jar, pour in the boiling water, and shake until well blended. This mixture will also come in handy for Moroccan cooking.

If you have time to marinate the fish: Pour ¼ cup (2 fl oz/ 60 ml) of the paprika oil into a large sauté pan. Add the garlic, cilantro stems, bell peppers, and chiles. Place the grouper on top and add the preserved lemons. Pour 3 tablespoons of the saffron water evenly over the fish. Use your hands to rub the liquids into the fish. Season with salt and pepper. If you have time, cover the pan and let the fish marinate in the fridge for up to 24 hours.

Remove the pan from the fridge, place over medium-high heat, and cook, covered, for 10 minutes. Reduce the heat to low, sprinkle the cilantro leaves over the fish, and cook, uncovered, for 10 minutes longer. The dish should look bright and bubbly. Serve right away.

If you have don't have time to marinate the fish: Pour ¼ cup (2 fl oz/60 ml) of the paprika oil into a large sauté pan. Add the garlic, cilantro stems, bell peppers, and chiles, place over medium-high heat, and cook, stirring occasionally, until the peppers and chiles are softened, about 4 minutes.

Place the fish on top and add the preserved lemons. Pour 3 tablespoons of the saffron water evenly over the fish. Season with salt and pepper. Tilt the pan so that the liquids are evenly coating all of the fillets. Cover and cook over medium-high heat for 10 minutes. Reduce the heat to low, sprinkle the cilantro leaves over the fish, and cook, uncovered, for 10 minutes longer. The dish should look bright and bubbly. Serve right away.

Serves 6

lazy but crispy fish

I call this "lazy fish" because it's the perfect recipe to make on a lazy day. You aren't the only one who gets tired of cooking, trust me. This recipe has become a weekly staple in my household. Choose any thick-fleshed fish fillet you like, coat it with a simple crumb topping, and roast it for no more than several minutes. The golden crumbs include a mixture of cornflake crumbs, panko, lemon, and a hint of sun-dried tomato. This is definitely a crowd-pleaser. Serve it with a tossed salad and dinner is set. I love making this dish for a party because it doesn't take long to prepare and everyone likes it. You can make the crumbs ahead of time and store them in the fridge, so they are ready to go when you need them. Then pick up some fresh fish and you're ready to roll.

1   thick-fleshed, skin-on fish fillet, such as salmon, arctic char, halibut, flounder, or sea bass, about 2 lb (1 kg)

Silan (date syrup), pure maple syrup, agave nectar, or pure raw honey for drizzling

Yellow mustard for drizzling

1   cup (3 oz/90 g) Lazy Crumb Topping (page 35)

Preheat the oven to 375°F (190°C). Line a baking sheet with parchment paper.

Place the fish, skin side down, on the prepared baking sheet. Drizzle a little *silan* and mustard on the fish and rub them in using your fingers. Sprinkle with a thick layer of the crumb topping.

Roast until the fish is just cooked through, about 12 minutes,depending on the thickness of the fillet. To test for doneness, use a sharp knife to cut through the crumb topping, peek into the center of the fillet to see if it's opaque, and then cover up the slit with more crumbs. Serve right away or let cool and serve at room temperature.

Serves 4–6

arctic char with wasabi-mirin sauce over rice noodles

This recipe fulfills my fantasies—food fantasies, that is. Some folks like their fish slightly undercooked or even raw. I'm more than happy with a piece of charred fish. The corner piece that's been overcooked with the crispy skin is what I go for. And I also love spicy food—the spicier, the better. So you need to know that this recipe may not be for everybody (definitely not for kids). But if you like the sound of overcooked char served atop sticky rice noodles, all doused with a burning wasabi sweet sauce (I suggest 1 teaspoon for mild heat, 2 teaspoons for medium, and 2 tablespoons for blow-your-head-off heat!), you'll become addicted to this recipe. It's perfect with a cold beer or a glass of crisp white wine.

2	skin-on filleted sides of arctic char, about 3 lb (1.5 kg) total weight
1	package (1 lb/500 g) dried rice vermicelli
¼	cup (2 fl oz/60 ml) mirin
¼	cup (2 fl oz/60 ml) rice vinegar
2	tablespoons soy sauce
1–3	tablespoons wasabi paste (I use the squeeze type)
15	fresh basil leaves

Preheat the broiler.

Place the arctic char on a baking sheet and set it on the middle rack in the oven. Broil until the fish is light pink and the flesh appears dry, even slightly charred, about 9 minutes. Let cool for about 5 minutes.

Meanwhile, cook the rice noodles according to the package instructions. Drain and set aside.

In a small bowl, whisk together the mirin, vinegar, soy sauce, and wasabi paste until blended.

Place the noodles on a large platter and top with the fish. Drizzle the sauce evenly over the fish and noodles and scatter the basil leaves on top.

Serves 6

grilled fish with dill-yogurt sauce

If you don't have an outdoor grill, use a grill pan on your stove top to achieve a similar effect. For the best results, serve the fish the moment it comes off the grill. I suggest trying salmon or halibut steaks instead of fillets for a change of pace. This dish is great with basmati rice.

1½	cups (12 oz/375 g) plain Greek yogurt
½	cup (¾ oz/20 g) roughly chopped fresh dill
	Juice of ½ lemon
¼	cup (1 oz/30 g) roughly chopped pecans
	Kosher salt and freshly ground pepper
2	tablespoons pure raw honey or agave nectar
	Extra-virgin olive oil for brushing
4–6	fish steaks or thick fillets, about ½ lb (250 g) each

In a bowl, stir together the yogurt, dill, lemon juice, and pecans. Season with salt and pepper and stir to combine. Drizzle the honey over the top. Refrigerate until ready to serve.

Prepare a hot fire in a charcoal or gas grill.

Brush a tiny drop of oil over both sides of each fish steak and season both sides with salt and pepper. Grill the fish, turning once, until opaque at the center when tested with the tip of a knife, about 4 minutes per side. Transfer to warmed individual plates and top each steak with a dollop of the dill-yogurt sauce. Serve right away.

Serves 4–6

halibut stuffed with kale & feta pesto

Instead of marinating the halibut fillets, which many recipes call for, I cut slits into the top of each fillet and stuff them with a pesto made from kale, scallions, celery, and feta. My family and friends regularly request this clever, superb-tasting dish.

1	teaspoon grapeseed oil
6	skinless halibut fillets, about 6 oz (185 g) each
	Kosher salt and freshly ground pepper
2	scallions, white and pale green parts, each cut crosswise into 4 equal pieces
2	cups (4½ oz/140 g) coarsely chopped stemmed kale
1	rib celery, coarsely chopped
¼	cup (1¼ oz/40 g) crumbled feta cheese
1–2	tablespoons extra-virgin olive oil

Preheat the oven to 450°F (230°C). Using the grapeseed oil, lightly grease a rectangular baking dish large enough to accommodate the fillets in a single layer.

Place the halibut fillets in the prepared baking dish and season lightly with salt and pepper. Use a sharp knife to slash several deep cuts in the top of each fillet, being careful not to cut all the way through the fish.

In a mini food processor, combine the scallions, kale, celery, and cheese and process until the ingredients are crumb sized. Add 1 tablespoon of the olive oil and pulse until a paste forms, adding more oil as needed to achieve a good consistency. Season with salt and pepper.

Use a small spoon or your finger to stuff the pesto into the slits in each fillet, filling them with as much pesto as will fit and allowing it to overflow. Roast until the fish is opaque at the center when tested with the tip of a knife, about 15 minutes. Let cool for 3 minutes before serving.

Serves 6

miso-tahini glazed cod

I'm a salty-sweet kind of a girl. That's why I love this miso-tahini combination. These distinct flavors fuse together to create a light but surprisingly delicious blend, perfect for topping cod or any other mild-tasting fish. The miso-tahini glaze can be prepared up to 4 days in advance and stored in the fridge until ready to use. I also use this glaze as a dip for crudités, or I drizzle it over grilled eggplant or roasted carrots to change things up.

1	teaspoon grapeseed oil
6	skinless cod fillets, about 6 oz (185 g) each
	Kosher salt and freshly ground pepper
2	tablespoons white miso
⅓	cup (3½ oz/105 g) tahini
3	tablespoons pure maple syrup
1	teaspoon grated lemon zest
	Juice of ½ lemon
	Chopped fresh cilantro for garnish

Preheat the oven to 425°F (220°C). Using the grapeseed oil, lightly grease a baking sheet or a baking dish large enough to accommodate the fillets in a single layer.

Place the cod on the prepared baking sheet, and season with ¼ teaspoon each salt and pepper.

In a small bowl, whisk together the miso, tahini, maple syrup, and lemon zest and juice until blended. Generously brush the mixture over the cod. Roast until the fish is opaque at the center when tested with the tip of a knife and feels firm to the touch, about 10 minutes. Let cool for 5 minutes, then garnish with the cilantro and serve right away.

Serves 6

tamari salmon with edamame

When friends are coming over for dinner, this is the recipe they often request. It's easy to make: simply cook the salmon at a high temperature, pour the garlic-tamari sauce over the fillet, and sprinkle the crunchy, bright edamame on top. My kids fight for the edamame smothered in the zesty sauce. Tamari is traditionally a by-product of miso production and, unlike soy sauce, contains little or no wheat. It is also darker, thicker, and less salty than soy sauce. You'll find it in most supermarkets.

1	skinless salmon fillet, about 2 lb (1 kg)
	Kosher salt and freshly ground pepper
2	cloves garlic, minced
½	cup (4 fl oz/125 ml) tamari sauce
	Juice of ½ orange
3	tablespoons pure raw honey
½	teaspoon toasted sesame oil
3	tablespoons sesame seeds
1½	cups (7½ oz/235 g) frozen shelled edamame, thawed and brought to room temperature

Preheat the oven to 450°F (230°C). Line a baking sheet with parchment paper.

Place the salmon on the prepared baking sheet and season lightly with salt and pepper. Cover the pan with aluminum foil, place in the oven, and cook until the flesh flakes when prodded with a knife but is still moist or to your liking, 10–15 minutes. Remove from the oven, uncover, let cool for 15 minutes, and then transfer to a serving platter.

Meanwhile, in a glass jar, combine the garlic, tamari, orange juice, honey, and sesame oil and shake until well blended. Rinse the edamame under running warm water.

Pour the sauce over the cooled fish and sprinkle the edamame and sesame seeds evenly over the top. Serve right away. (That's right, the edamame don't need to be cooked. They were cooked before they were packaged and need only to be thawed.)

Serves 4–6

thai-style summer salmon

Here, the fish is cooked in a moderate oven, then drizzled with a gorgeous citrusy ginger-soy dressing and topped with lots of chopped cilantro, mint, and salted peanuts. This casual salmon dish is perfect for a summer gathering and goes together quickly. Use any leftover salmon on top of a mixed green salad or stuffed into pitas for a brilliant lunch.

1	teaspoon grapeseed oil
1	skinless salmon fillet, about 1½ lb (750 g)
⅓	cup (3 fl oz/80 ml) soy sauce
¼	cup (2 fl oz/60 ml) fresh orange juice
1½	tablespoons peeled and minced fresh ginger
3	tablespoons plum sauce or duck sauce
2	tablespoons pure maple syrup
2	tablespoons roughly chopped fresh cilantro
2	tablespoons roughly chopped fresh mint
3	tablespoons roughly chopped salted peanuts

Preheat the oven to 375°F (190°C). Using the grapeseed oil, lightly grease a baking dish large enough to accommodate the salmon fillet.

Place the fish in the prepared baking dish. Cover with aluminum foil, place in the oven, and cook until the flesh flakes when prodded with a knife but is still moist or to your liking, 15–20 minutes. Remove from the oven, uncover, let cool for 5 minutes, and transfer to a serving platter.

Meanwhile, in a small bowl, whisk together the soy sauce, orange juice, ginger, plum sauce, and maple syrup until well blended.

Spoon the sauce over the fish, sprinkle with the cilantro, mint, and peanuts, and serve right away.

Serves 4–6

seared tuna with sun-dried tomato & jalapeño preserves

This seared tuna makes a striking, sophisticated main course. The spicy preserves are bursting with layers of flavors from the bold sun-dried tomatoes, the zesty basil, and the sharp garlic. I often prepare the preserves a day or two in advance and store them in the fridge. I also like to serve this dish as an appetizer by reducing the quantity of tuna. (I still make the same amount of preserves, however, as they always get devoured!) For less spicy preserves, remove and discard the seeds from the jalapeño. If you have more preserves than you need for this dish, they will keep in a tightly capped jar in the fridge for up to one week. Just be sure to serve them at room temperature, not straight out of the fridge.

½	cup (2½ oz/75 g) drained oil-packed or (1½ oz/45 g) dry-packed sun-dried tomatoes
2	cups (2 oz/60 g) fresh basil leaves
1	handful fresh mint leaves
1	jalapeño chile, stemmed and halved lengthwise
1	large clove garlic
3–4	tablespoons extra-virgin olive oil
1	tablespoon balsamic vinegar
	Kosher salt and freshly ground pepper
6	tuna steaks, about 6 oz (185 g) each, cut into 2-by-4-inch (5-by-10-cm) pieces
1	tablespoon neutral oil such as avocado, sunflower, or canola

In a food processor, combine the sun-dried tomatoes, basil, mint, jalapeño, and garlic and pulse until the ingredients are finely chopped. Add 3 tablespoons of the olive oil, the vinegar, and ¼ teaspoon each salt and pepper and process for a few seconds to combine, adding more oil if needed to achieve a good consistency. Transfer the preserves to a bowl or glass jar and set aside.

Season the tuna with salt and pepper. In a large sauté pan, heat the neutral oil over high heat. Working in batches to avoid crowding, add the tuna and sear, turning once, for 1 minute per side. Transfer to a cutting board and let rest for 3 minutes. Cut the tuna against the grain into thin slices.

Arrange the tuna slices on a serving plater and drizzle with the preserves. Serve at room temperature.

Serves 6

all
about
chicken

red roast chicken with lemon, whole garlic & vegetables

There's never a bite left when I make this simple yet spectacular roast chicken. I cook it on a chicken stand (an empty soda or beer can works, too), which holds the bird upright while it roasts. The result is crisp, golden skin and moist meat. It's the best cooking invention ever. I stuff the cavity with lemon halves and fresh thyme, then surround the chicken with vegetables on a parchment-lined baking dish, so cleanup is fast and easy. It cooks perfectly, and the vegetables turn into caramelized goodness. Look for a chicken stand at cookware stores and online.

1	head garlic
1	teaspoon extra-virgin olive oil, plus more for drizzling
1	lemon
1	chicken, about 3½ lb (1.75 kg)
	Kosher salt and freshly ground pepper
1	bunch fresh thyme
1	tablespoon sweet paprika or sumac
1	teaspoon dried basil
5	carrots, peeled and sliced
1	zucchini, sliced
1	fennel bulb, trimmed, cored, and thinly sliced
1	handful of pearl onions, peeled

Preheat the oven to 400°F (200°C). Have a large roasting pan handy.

Cut 1 inch (2.5 cm) off the top of the garlic head; do not discard. Place both garlic pieces on a piece of aluminum foil and drizzle with the 1 teaspoon oil. Wrap the foil over the garlic, enclosing it completely. Set aside.

Cut the lemon in half and squeeze the juice into the cavity and over the outside of the chicken. Reserve the lemon halves. Generously season the cavity and the outside of the chicken with salt and pepper. Stuff the lemon halves and thyme inside the chicken, then place the chicken on a chicken stand. Sprinkle the paprika and basil over the outside of the chicken, using your hands to spread them all over. Place the stand with the chicken in the roasting pan. Surround with the carrots, zucchini, fennel, and onions. Place the foil-wrapped garlic in the pan. Drizzle a little bit of oil over the vegetables.

Roast for 1 hour. Reduce the oven temperature to 325°F (165°C) and roast until the chicken is golden brown and the juices run clear when a skewer is inserted into the thickest part of the thigh, about 1 hour longer. (If you would like to keep the chicken and vegetables warm, turn off the oven then keep them in the warm oven for up to 1 hour longer.)

Once the chicken is cool enough to handle, take it off the stand and discard the lemon halves and thyme. Cut the chicken into serving pieces. Unwrap the garlic and squeeze the cloves over the chicken to release the golden, roasted deliciousness. Transfer the chicken and vegetables to a serving platter. Now, devour.

Serves 4–6

grilled chicken verte

People often ask me for skinless, boneless chicken breast recipes. I think that home cooks are searching for some out-of-this-world recipe, but I always say, "The simpler, the better!" Here is a wonderful dish that basically uses whatever fresh herbs I have left over in my fridge, plus chopped garlic, olive oil, and a splash of balsamic vinegar. That's pretty much it. Literally.

2	cups (2 oz/60 g) fresh herb leaves, such as flat-leaf parsley, mint, cilantro, dill, and/or basil
3	cloves garlic
3	tablespoons extra-virgin olive oil
	Splash of balsamic vinegar
	Kosher salt and freshly ground pepper
6	chicken cutlets, about 1½ lb (750 g) total weight, pounded about ⅛–¼ inch (3–6 mm) thick
	Lemon wedges for serving

In a mini food processor, combine the herbs and garlic and process until finely chopped. Add the oil and vinegar and process until combined. Season with salt and pepper.

Place the chicken cutlets in a large lock-top plastic bag, pour the marinade into the bag, and seal the bag. Marinate for at least 10 minutes on the countertop or for up to 24 hours in the fridge.

Prepare a medium-hot fire in a charcoal or gas grill.

Remove the chicken from the bag and shake off any excess marinade. Grill the chicken, turning once, until cooked through, about 3 minutes per side. Serve right away, accompanied with the lemon wedges.

Serves 4–6

chicken & dill stew

This stew is an old family favorite of mine. My mom makes it all the time, and it's one of those "you can't screw it up" recipes. It's perfect to serve in the fall and winter and can be prepared in under a half hour. Skinless, boneless chicken breasts are cut into fingerlike strips and smothered in sautéed onions and a ketchup-soy blend. When the chicken is cooked and the sauce has thickened, chopped fresh dill is tossed in. The dill is what takes the dish to the next level, adding a rich, robust flavor. The stew goes well with steamed rice, roasted potatoes, or even pasta. Because it reheats wonderfully, it can be made a day or two in advance.

2	tablespoons extra-virgin olive oil
4	yellow onions, about 1½ lb (750 g) each, thinly sliced
8	skinless, boneless chicken breast halves, about 2 lb (1 kg) total weight, cut against the grain into fingerlike strips
1	cup (8 oz/250 g) tomato ketchup
½	cup (4 fl oz/125 ml) soy sauce
1	bay leaf
¼	teaspoon freshly ground pepper
2	handfuls of chopped fresh dill

In a large sauté pan, heat the oil over medium-high heat. Add the onions and cook, stirring occasionally, until translucent, about 10 minutes. Add the chicken and cook, stirring occasionally, for 5 minutes.

Meanwhile, in a small bowl, whisk together the ketchup and soy sauce. When the chicken has cooked for 5 minutes, pour in the ketchup-soy mixture, add the bay leaf and pepper, and stir well. Reduce the heat to medium, cover, and cook until the chicken is cooked through and the sauce has thickened, 10–15 minutes.

Remove from the heat, uncover, and toss in the dill. Re-cover and let the stew stand for about 5 minutes to allow the flavors to deepen. Remove and discard the bay leaf. That's it!

Serves 6–8

lime & sesame-soy chicken

This chicken recipe is a great one: zesty, crisp, and with just a touch of sweetness. Fresh lime juice really brings out the sunshine, and a sprinkle of sesame seeds makes the dish taste good and look beautiful. If you can get your hands on fresh bay leaves, use them in the marinade. The chicken turns out perfectly whether it's cooked on a grill or in the oven. Use any cut of chicken that you like. Serve with grilled vegetables and an ice-cold beer.

1	chicken, about 3½ lb (1.75 kg), cut into 8–10 pieces, or 8–10 bone-in chicken pieces of your choice, about 3 lb (1.5 kg) total weight (skin on or skinless)
1	tablespoon onion powder
	Juice of 2 limes
¼	cup (2 fl oz/60 ml) soy sauce
2	tablespoons peach or apricot preserves
2	bay leaves
2	tablespoons sesame seeds

Place the chicken in a large bowl and sprinkle with the onion powder. Add the lime juice, soy sauce, and preserves and use your hands to combine well, coating each piece evenly. Add the bay leaves and sprinkle the sesame seeds evenly over the top. Cover and marinate at room temperature for 30 minutes or in the fridge for up to 24 hours. Remove and discard the bay leaves before cooking.

If grilling outdoors: Prepare a hot fire in a charcoal or gas grill. Scrape any excess marinade off the chicken. Grill the chicken, turning once, until cooked through, about 5 minutes per side. Serve hot or at room temperature.

If cooking indoors: Preheat the oven to 375°F (190°C). Arrange the chicken in a single layer in a roasting pan and add any marinade. Roast uncovered for about 45 minutes. Turn the chicken pieces over and continue to roast until cooked through, about 30 minutes longer. Serve hot or at room temperature.

Serves 6

chicken potpies

This is a recipe that you'd assume would be complicated, yet it is anything but! It's actually fast and simple, with results that are guaranteed to please. You can use store-bought rotisserie chicken or leftover home-cooked chicken of any kind, and the flaky pie topping is made with purchased puff pastry. Peel the meat off the bones, discard the bones and skin, and chop the meat into small pieces. I like a mix of dark and white meat, but use whatever you have. My neighbors are trying to convince me to market my potpies. Until I get around to doing that, here's the recipe. Add any vegetables you'd like along with the ones here.

4	tablespoons extra-virgin olive oil
1	large yellow onion, diced
4	carrots, about 1 lb (500 g) total weight, peeled and diced
3	ribs celery, diced
1–2	handfuls of white mushrooms, diced
1	cup (5 oz/155 g) frozen peas
2–3	cups (12–18 oz/375–560 g) shredded cooked chicken pieces, cut into small pieces
2	cups (16 fl oz/500 ml) chicken or vegetable stock
	Kosher salt and freshly ground pepper
2	tablespoons all-purpose flour
1	sheet frozen puff pastry, about ½ lb (250 g), thawed on the countertop for 15 minutes
1	large egg, beaten

In a large sauté pan, heat 2 tablespoons of the oil over medium heat. Add the onion and cook, stirring occasionally, until it begins to soften, about 3 minutes. Add the carrots and celery and cook, stirring occasionally, until softened, about 10 minutes. Add the mushrooms and cook for 2 minutes longer. Then add the peas, chicken, and stock and season generously with salt and pepper. Raise the heat to medium-high, and heat until the mixture is bubbly and starts to thicken.

In a small bowl, whisk together the flour and the remaining 2 tablespoons oil until well combined, creating a roux. Whisk the roux into the sauté pan and cook, stirring occasionally, for 10 minutes. The roux will act as a thickener and will also give the mixture a velvety texture. The final result should be a thick filling with vegetables and chicken. If it isn't thick enough, continue to cook over high heat for 5 minutes longer. (You can make this part of the recipe in advance. Let cool, then cover and store in the fridge for up to 2 days until ready to assemble the potpies.)

Preheat the oven to 375°F (190°C). Have ready eight ½-cup (4–fl oz/125-ml) ramekins.

Roll out the puff pastry so that it is slightly larger than its original size. Using an overturned ramekin as a template, cut out 8 rounds from the pastry sheet, making them just slightly larger than the diameter of the ramekin. Divide the chicken filling evenly among the 8 ramekins, filling them to the top. Place a pastry round atop each ramekin and press down on the edges to adhere to the rim. Use a sharp knife to cut a few small slits in the top of each pastry round (this will let the steam out). Brush the pastry with the egg wash and place the ramekins on a large foil-lined baking sheet (to catch any leaks).

Bake until golden and gorgeous, 15–20 minutes. Serve hot. The potpies can be baked ahead of time and refrigerated for up to 48 hours. Reheat in a 350°F (180°C) oven for 10 minutes before serving.

Serves 8

all-in-one turkey rice bowl

This is one of my kids' all-time favorite dinners. It's a one-pot rice dish made with ground turkey, but feel free to substitute ground beef, lamb, chicken, or crumbled tofu. Reminiscent of Spanish-style rice, the dish includes onions, tomatoes, and red and green bell peppers. I serve it in bowls, which makes the kids really happy (I have no idea why). And if there are no kids involved, you can have even more fun by topping the rice bowl with your favorite hot sauce, the Red Chimichurri Sauce on page 77, raw onions, or whatever you like.

2	tablespoons extra-virgin olive oil
1	large yellow onion, finely diced
2	ribs celery, finely diced
1	lb (500 g) ground turkey
1	red bell pepper, seeded and finely diced
1	green bell pepper, seeded and finely diced
1	can (15 oz/470 g) diced or crushed tomatoes, with juices
	Kosher salt and freshly ground pepper
1	teaspoon dried basil
2	tablespoons rice vinegar
1	cup (7 oz/220 g) white basmati or long-grain rice

In a large sauté pan, heat the oil over medium-high heat. Add the onion and cook, stirring occasionally, until translucent, about 3 minutes. Add the celery and ground turkey and cook, using a wooden spoon to break up the meat into tiny pieces, about 8 minutes.

Add the bell peppers and tomatoes and juice and cook, stirring occasionally, for 2 minutes longer. Season generously with salt and pepper. Stir in the basil, vinegar, and rice and bring to a boil. Reduce the heat to medium-low, cover, and cook, stirring once after about 15 minutes, until the rice is tender and the flavors are blended, about 30 minutes. Serve right away.

Serves 4–6

quick chicken & vegetables on the stove top

I love preparing chicken on the stove top because it cooks more quickly than it does in the oven and is less likely to dry out. By gently simmering bone-in or boneless chicken pieces in a sauce, you are essentially braising them. This cooking technique is hard to mess up, and it's simple. First, I cut and sauté whatever vegetables I have on hand. Then I stir in tomatoes in two forms to make an aromatic sauce, add the chicken, and simmer everything together over low heat until the chicken is cooked. The result is always flavor packed and succulent. This is a great tried-and-true recipe that works with different vegetables and any cut of chicken. I like skin-on, bone-in thighs, but you can even use skinless, boneless chicken breasts cut into strips. The beauty of this recipe is its simplicity. It's a wonderful dish to serve family style for a dinner party.

3	carrots, peeled
2	teaspoons extra-virgin olive oil
2	zucchini, finely diced
	Kosher salt and freshly ground pepper
1	cup (6 oz/185 g) cherry tomatoes, halved
1	cup (6 oz/185 g) frozen corn kernels
1	cup (8 fl oz/250 ml) tomato sauce
1	clove garlic, minced
8	chicken pieces of your choice, about 3½ lb (1.75 kg) total weight if bone-in or about 3 lb (1.5 kg) total weight if boneless (skin-on or skinless)
2	tablespoons sweet paprika
1	teaspoon ground turmeric
1	teaspoon dried basil

Use a vegetable peeler to cut the carrots lengthwise into long, thin ribbons.

In a large sauté pan with a tight-fitting lid, heat the oil over medium-high heat. Add the carrots and zucchini and season with salt and pepper. Cover and cook, stirring occasionally, until softened, about 10 minutes. Add the tomatoes and corn and cook for 5 minutes longer. Add the tomato sauce and garlic and stir well.

Meanwhile, place the chicken in a large bowl and sprinkle with the paprika, turmeric, and basil. Use your hands to rub the spices into each piece. Season with salt and pepper. Transfer the chicken to the pan and scoop the vegetables and sauce over the pieces until well coated. Bring to a boil, reduce the heat to medium-low, cover, and simmer until the chicken is cooked through. Boneless chicken breasts will take 20–25 minutes; larger bone-in pieces can take up to 1 hour. Transfer the chicken to a warmed platter and spoon the vegetables and sauce over the top. Serve right away.

Serves 6–8

chicken-spinach burgers

Looking for a quick and easy dinner recipe that will satisfy everyone at the table? I always am. I love this recipe for chicken-spinach burgers (you can swap in ground beef or turkey, if you like). Flavored with a touch of nutmeg and a little Worcestershire sauce, these burgers please all palates, big and small. I use thawed frozen chopped spinach and blend it into the meat mixture. It's a great way to add some vegetables to your meal. I like to make mini burgers, and everyone in my house pops them like hotcakes. You can cook them ahead of time and freeze them so they are easy to thaw and reheat for dinner.

1½	lb (750 g) ground chicken (dark or white meat)
1	package (10 oz/315 g) frozen chopped spinach, thawed and squeezed of excess liquid
1	large egg
½	teaspoon ground nutmeg
1	teaspoon Worcestershire sauce
3	tablespoons tomato ketchup or tomato paste
¼	cup (1 oz/30 g) dried bread crumbs or (½ oz/15 g) panko
	Kosher salt and freshly ground pepper

In a large bowl, combine the chicken, spinach, egg, nutmeg, Worcestershire sauce, ketchup, bread crumbs, 1 teaspoon salt, and ½ teaspoon pepper. Use your hands to mix thoroughly. Cover and refrigerate for 15 minutes to allow the mixture to firm up.

Form the meat mixture into small patties, using about ¼ cup (2 oz/60 g) of the meat mixture per patty and making each patty about 2½ inches (6 cm) thick. If the mixture is super sticky, wet your hands before forming the patties.

If cooking indoors: Preheat the oven to 450°F (230°C). Place the patties on a baking sheet. Roast until cooked through, about 20 minutes. If you have a stove-top grill pan, you can grill them over medium-high heat for 1–2 minutes on each side, just to get some nice grill marks, and then finish cooking them in a 400°F (200°C) oven for about 12 minutes. That's what I do.

If grilling outdoors: Prepare a medium-hot fire in a charcoal or gas grill. Grill the burgers, turning once, until cooked through, about 4 minutes per side. Serve the burgers right away.

Serves 6

autumn chicken ratatouille

I use peak-season fresh vegetables in this recipe—eggplant and yams—and combine them with chicken pieces in a large sauté pan on the stove top. I season the chicken with basil, dry mustard, cinnamon, and a splash of cider vinegar that adds just the right amount of tang. The result is a silky vegetable ratatouille surrounding hearty pieces of chicken. It's a dinner that everyone in the family will enjoy (I even purée this dish for the baby), and it can even be cooked in advance and reheated for lunch or dinner the next day.

2	tablespoons olive oil
1	large yellow onion, diced
3	Garnet yams, peeled and cut into small cubes
1	eggplant, peeled or unpeeled, cut into small cubes
	Kosher salt and freshly ground pepper
1	chicken, about 3½ lb (1.75 kg), cut into 8–10 pieces, or 8 bone-in chicken pieces of your choice, about 3 lb (1.5 kg) total weight (skin on or skinless)
1	teaspoon dried basil
1	teaspoon dry mustard
1	teaspoon ground cinnamon
¼	cup (2 fl oz/60 ml) apple cider vinegar

In a large sauté pan with a tight-fitting lid, heat the oil over medium-high heat. Add the onion and cook, stirring occasionally, until translucent, about 3 minutes. Add the yams and eggplant and season with ½ teaspoon salt and ¼ teaspoon pepper. Reduce the heat to medium and cook, covered, until the vegetables are softened, 10–15 minutes.

Meanwhile, place the chicken in a large bowl and sprinkle with the basil, mustard, cinnamon, and vinegar. Use your hands to rub the spices and vinegar into each piece.

Add the chicken to the pan, scoop the vegetables over the chicken, and pour in ¼ cup (2 fl oz/60 ml) water. Bring to a boil, reduce the heat to medium-low, cover, and simmer until the chicken is cooked through, 35–45 minutes.

Serve the chicken and vegetables right out of the pan, or let cool, cover, and refrigerate for up to 1 day, then reheat gently just before serving.

Serves 6–8

kim's sticky chicky with potatoes

This recipe has been one of the most sought-after on my blog. Every time I have posted a picture of this scrumptious sticky chicky, the response has been wild. So finally, I am sharing it with you. This is a recipe that you will memorize, master, and make time and time again. Don't be afraid of the indefinite measurements. The beauty of this dish is that it can be thrown together quickly, with a squirt here and a drizzle there. I use any potatoes I have on hand, including sweet potatoes (yams) and small potatoes, and often I mix them. This is the way dinner was meant to be—fast, flexible, and delicious.

8	skin-on, bone-in chicken pieces of your choice, about 3 lb (1.5 kg) total weight
1	yellow onion, chopped
4–6	potatoes (any variety, including Garnet yams), about 1½ lb (750 g) total weight, peeled and cut into wedges
	Kosher salt and freshly ground pepper
1	big squirt of tomato ketchup
1	squirt of honey
3	tablespoons soy sauce
1	tablespoon Worcestershire sauce

Preheat the oven to 400°F (200°C).

Place the chicken, onion, and potatoes in a roasting pan or a rectangular baking dish and season with salt and pepper. Add the ketchup, honey, soy sauce, and Worcestershire sauce, then use your hands to slather them evenly over the chicken and potatoes.

Cover the pan with aluminum foil and place in the oven for 30 minutes. Uncover the pan, reduce the oven temperature to 325°F (165°C), and continue to cook until the chicken is golden brown, sticky, and perfect, about 2 hours longer. Serve right away.

Serves 4–6

slow-cooked chicken with fennel & white wine

I feel that too many people are afraid to give fennel a fair shot. If you're on the fence, give this recipe a try. The garlic and fennel are caramelized, so the fennel's distinct "licorice" flavor is mellowed, and the white wine adds the ideal note of acidity. If you love fennel like I do, this will become your go-to chicken recipe.

1	chicken, about 3½ lb (1.75 kg), cut into 8 pieces, or 8 bone-in chicken pieces of your choice, about 3 lb (1.5 kg) total weight (skin on or skinless)
6	cloves garlic, minced
2	fennel bulbs, trimmed, cored, and thinly sliced
1	cup (1 oz/30 g) fresh flat-leaf parsley leaves, minced
1	cup (8 fl oz/250 ml) dry white wine
	Juice of 1 lemon
	Kosher salt and freshly ground pepper
1	cup (5 oz/155 g) frozen baby peas

Place the chicken in a roasting pan. Add the garlic, fennel, parsley, wine, lemon juice, ½ teaspoon salt, and ¼ teaspoon pepper and use your hands to mix well. Marinate at room temperature for 10 minutes or cover and marinate in the fridge for up to 24 hours.

Preheat the oven to 400°F (200°C).

Roast the chicken for 20 minutes. Reduce the oven temperature to 300°F (150°C) and continue to roast for 1 hour and 40 minutes longer, basting with the pan juices twice during cooking. Sprinkle the peas into the pan and continue to roast until the chicken is golden and crisp, about 20 minutes longer. Serve right away.

Serves 4–6

braised beef short ribs with cider-herb reduction

Some home cooks think that cooking beef short ribs requires a culinary degree, but they're totally mistaken. Tender, succulent ribs are one of the easiest meats to cook. This simple recipe yields slow-cooked ribs that are flavorful and finger-licking, falling-off-the-bone good. The sharpness of the cider vinegar in the sauce is contrasted with the sweetness of just a touch of honey. Look for flanken-style short ribs, which are ribs that have been cut across the bone, with each piece containing three or four small bone sections and lots of meat. This dish is a great example of how, when it comes to cooking, less is often more. You don't need dozens of ingredients to make an amazing dish. There's even a good chance you already have everything you'll need for this dish in your pantry. Just go out and get yourself some ribs!

6	flanken-style short ribs, about 2½ lb (1.25 kg) total weight
	Kosher salt and freshly ground pepper
4	cloves garlic, minced
½	cup (4 fl oz/125 ml) cider vinegar
1	can (6 oz/185 g) tomato paste
½	cup (4 fl oz/125 ml) dry red wine
1	tablespoon dried oregano
1	tablespoon dried basil
1	heaping tablespoon pure raw honey
1	teaspoon extra-virgin olive oil

Preheat the oven to 400°F (200°C).

Season the short ribs with ½ teaspoon salt and ¼ teaspoon pepper and then rub the ribs with the garlic. Place the ribs in a single layer in a large baking dish or pan.

In a bowl, whisk together the vinegar, tomato paste, wine, oregano, basil, honey, and oil. Pour the marinade over the ribs. You can cover and marinate in the fridge overnight or cook straightaway.

Cover the baking dish with aluminum foil and transfer to the oven. Immediately reduce the oven temperature to 350°F (180°C) and cook for 2½ hours. Turn the oven off but keep the ribs in the oven for 1 hour longer (they will really soften up during this time!).

Remove the ribs from the oven and serve right away. Alternatively, let cool completely, transfer to an airtight container, and refrigerate for up to 4 days or freeze for up to 1 month. If frozen, thaw overnight in the fridge. To serve, reheat in a preheated 300°F (150°C) oven until hot. That's it. How easy is that?

Serves 6

london broil with maple & soy

I am a steak and potatoes kind of girl. I will never turn away a good steak! But let's get real: when it comes to dinner parties and barbecues for a large crowd, how can you serve each person a rib eye without breaking the bank? There's a better way to serve steak. The answer is London broil, which is a cooking method rather than a cut. It calls for marinating a flank steak or a top round steak, grilling or broiling it, and then thinly slicing it. The maple and soy combination here is tangy, salty, and sweet. I like using this cooking method because when I slice the meat after taking it off the grill, I can take half of the medium-rare slices and cook them a little longer in the oven until they are medium-well. That way, everyone in my family is satisfied.

¼	cup (2 fl oz/60 ml) extra-virgin olive oil
½	cup (4 fl oz/125 ml) soy sauce
3	tablespoons pure maple syrup
2	tablespoons dried rosemary
1	teaspoon orange zest
	Freshly ground pepper
1	flank or top round steak for London broil, about 2½ lb (1.25 kg)
1	large red onion, thinly sliced

In a bowl, whisk together the oil, soy sauce, maple syrup, rosemary, orange zest, and ½ teaspoon pepper.

Place the meat and onion in a large lock-top plastic bag, pour the marinade into the bag, and seal the bag. Marinate in the fridge for at least 30 minutes or up to 2 days.

Prepare a hot fire in a charcoal or gas grill, or preheat a stove-top grill pan over high heat. Preheat the oven to 350°F (180°C).

Remove the meat from the bag and shake off the excess marinade. Reserve the marinade. Grill the meat, turning once, until nicely charred on both sides, about 5 minutes per side. The meat will be medium-rare. Transfer to a cutting board and let rest for about 10 minutes.

Cut the meat against the grain into slices ¼ inch (6 mm) thick.

To cook some of the meat medium-well, place the slices in a baking dish and pour the reserved marinade over the top. Cover with aluminum foil, transfer to the oven, and cook for 10 minutes. Remove from the oven and serve immediately.

Serves 4–6

grilled steak with caramelized tandoori peppers

How do you find the time to prepare gourmet meals every night of the week? is a question that I am often asked. My answer is usually the same: simple is always best, make what you can in advance, and the most delicious flavors come from the freshest ingredients. A dish doesn't have to be fancy, expensive, or time-consuming. Grilled meats taste great and are quick to prepare. If you're a fan of bold, hot flavors, try this recipe, which features tandoori bell peppers paired with steak. Tandoori masala powder, a spice blend created specifically for use with a tandoor, or clay oven, typically includes garam masala, garlic, ginger, onion, and cayenne pepper. You can buy it online, but I encourage you to go out and explore your local spice stores.

2	tablespoons extra-virgin olive oil
4	bell peppers (any color), about 1½ lb (750 g) total weight, seeded and thinly sliced
1	teaspoon curry powder
½	teaspoon tandoori masala powder
	Kosher salt and freshly ground pepper
1	flank steak, about 2½ lb (1.25 kg)

In a large sauté pan, heat the oil over low heat. Add the bell peppers and cook, stirring occasionally, until they shrink down, are deeply caramelized, and are almost sticking together, about 30 minutes. Stir in the curry powder and tandoori masala powder and season with salt and pepper. Remove from the heat and let cool. (The peppers will keep in an airtight container in the fridge for up to 1 week. Bring to room temperature before serving.)

Prepare a medium-hot fire in a charcoal or gas grill or preheat a stove-top grill pan over medium-high heat. Season the steak on both sides with salt and pepper. Grill the steak, turning once, until sizzling, about 7 minutes per side. Transfer to a cutting board and let rest for about 10 minutes.

Cut the steak against the grain into thin slices. Serve right away and accompany each serving with a dollop of the tandoori peppers.

Serves 6–8

winter minute steaks & potatoes

If you want steak and potatoes, you've got it with this easy, no-fail recipe. It is a good dish to make on a lazy winter day, and because it uses only a few pantry staples, it's a recipe that you will definitely want to bookmark.

8	minute steaks, about 3 lb (1.5 g) total weight, or 1 flank steak, about 2½ lb (1.25 kg)
	Kosher salt and freshly ground pepper
4	Yukon gold potatoes, about 1½ lb (750 g) total weight, cut into wedges
1	large yellow onion, thinly sliced
2	cups (16 fl oz/500 ml) marinara sauce
1	tablespoon soy sauce
1	teaspoon Worcestershire sauce

Preheat the oven to 350°F (180°C).

Season each steak on both sides with ¼ teaspoon each salt and pepper. Place the steaks in a single layer in a rectangular baking dish. Arrange the potato wedges and onion slices around the steaks. In a bowl, stir together the marinara sauce, soy sauce, Worcestershire, and ½ cup (4 fl oz/125 ml) water, mixing well, and then pour the mixture evenly over the contents of the baking dish.

Cover the baking dish with aluminum foil, place in the oven, and cook until the meat is tender enough to break up easily with a fork, 2–2½ hours.

Remove from the oven, serve immediately, and enjoy—the meat comes out like butter!

Serves 4–6

kim's bolognese sauce

Ragù alla bolognese, which originated in the city of Bologna in northern Italy, is traditionally made with ground beef, pork, and vegetables and is enhanced with milk and seasonings. So it's obvious why a kosher cook might have trouble duplicating an authentic Bolognese sauce. For years, I've perused kosher cookbooks searching for a great meat sauce recipe. What I usually found were versions loaded with ketchup and sugar—more sweet-and-sour than a truly hearty and full-bodied Bolognese. After a bit of experimentation and some mixing and matching, I found a way to achieve a gorgeously thick, rich-tasting, aromatic meat sauce. I also discovered a magical ingredient. A few years ago, I met a woman in Italy who told me the secret to her Bolognese came from her mother. When the sauce was done, she stirred in a tiny amount of good honey, just to release the sweetness. This takes the flavor from homemade to gourmet, and I love the results. When you try it, you'll understand.

2	tablespoons extra-virgin olive oil
3	yellow onions, thinly sliced
6	carrots, about 5 lb (2.5 kg) total weight, peeled and grated
3	ribs celery, grated
2	bay leaves
1	can (6 oz/185 g) tomato paste
3	cups (24 fl oz/750 ml) dry red wine (don't be cheap; use a wine you would enjoy drinking)
2½	lb (1.25 kg) ground beef
4	cans (15 oz/470 g each) crushed tomatoes, or 2 jars (26 oz/815 g each) marinara sauce
1	tablespoon dried basil
	Kosher salt and freshly ground pepper
1	teaspoon pure raw honey

In a large pot, heat the oil over medium-high heat. Add the onions and cook, stirring occasionally, until caramelized, about 15 minutes. Add the carrots, celery, and bay leaves, cover, and cook for 5 minutes.

Stir in the tomato paste, incorporating it into the vegetables, then stir in 2 cups (16 fl oz/500 ml) of the wine. Cook, uncovered, for 5 minutes. Crumble in the beef and, using a wooden spoon, stir it into the vegetables, breaking the meat apart into small pieces. Add in the tomatoes and bring to a boil. Cover partially and cook for 30 minutes, stirring often and continuing to break up the meat. Add the remaining 1 cup (8 fl oz/250 ml) wine and the basil and season generously with salt and pepper. Reduce the heat to medium, cover partially, and cook until the sauce has thickened to perfection, about 40 minutes longer.

Taste and adjust the seasoning to your liking. Remove and discard the bay leaves and stir in the honey. This recipe makes a huge quantity, but luckily the sauce freezes beautifully. (I use it in lasagne as well as over pasta.) Freeze it for for up to 1 month, thaw in the refrigerator overnight, and reheat over medium heat.

Makes about 2½ qt (2.5 l)

mini meatballs in cinnamon-tomato sauce

Meatballs have long been a staple of kosher cooking. I've grown tired of the oversweetened sweet-and-sour versions, but I still long for a thick and delicious sauce. Here, I add cinnamon and allspice to the sauce, which yields a warm, comforting flavor. I always form the meat mixture into teeny-tiny balls, for no reason other than kids love them that way. Perhaps little ones are more fun to eat! Whenever I am hosting a dinner party and I know that children will be attending, I fill ramekins with pasta and top them with these little meatballs, which always scores high with them. The meatballs and sauce can be frozen in an airtight container for up to a month. Thaw the meatballs in the fridge overnight, then reheat them gently over medium heat.

For the Sauce

3	cans (15 oz/470 g each) tomato sauce
2	cans (6 oz/185 g each) tomato paste
1	tablespoon fresh lemon juice
1	teaspoon sugar
½	teaspoon ground cinnamon
½	teaspoon ground allspice
	Kosher salt and freshly ground pepper

For the Meatballs

1½	lb (750 g) ground beef
1	large egg, beaten
⅓	cup (1 oz/30 g) cornflake crumbs
¼	teaspoon *each* ground nutmeg, ground cinnamon, and ground allspice
	Kosher salt and freshly ground pepper

To make the sauce, in a large sauté pan, stir together the tomato sauce and paste, lemon juice, sugar, cinnamon, allspice, ½ teaspoon salt, and ¼ teaspoon pepper. Place over medium heat and bring to a gentle simmer.

Meanwhile, make the meatballs: In a large bowl, combine the beef, egg, cornflake crumbs, nutmeg, cinnamon, allspice, 1 teaspoon salt, and ¼ teaspoon pepper and mix thoroughly with your hands. Dampen your hands and form the mixture into balls, using 1–2 teaspoons for each ball. As the balls are formed, add them to the sauce.

When all the meatballs are in the sauce, stir once, cover, and simmer gently for about 1½ hours, stirring every 30 minutes and adjusting the heat if needed to prevent scorching. The dish is ready when the sauce is thick and the meatballs are tender. Serve right away.

Makes about 48 mini meatballs

lamb rib chops with red wine vinegar, mint & garlic

When I was growing up, my mom always made lamb on Passover. It was a real treat, something we looked forward to all year. My siblings and I knew that lamb was a special dish, and we felt lucky and proud to have it. I now find myself making a big deal out of serving lamb to my family. Mom serves hers in a traditional Jewish Moroccan style with canned truffles. My recipe is more modern, but I can't say that it's better than hers! The lamb chops are marinated in a mixture of red wine vinegar, red wine, garlic, orange, mint, and cilantro, and the result is unbelievably good. Ask the butcher to french the lamb chops—remove any meat, cartilage, or fat from the tips of the bones—or you can do it yourself.

¼	cup (2 fl oz/60 ml) red wine vinegar
	Splash of dry red wine (plus a glass for yourself to enjoy while you're cooking; optional but recommended!)
¼	cup (2 fl oz/60 ml) extra-virgin olive oil
4	cloves garlic, crushed
1	orange
1	handful of fresh mint sprigs, stemmed and roughly chopped
1	handful of fresh cilantro sprigs, stemmed and roughly chopped
	Kosher salt and freshly ground pepper
12	lamb rib chops, about 4 lb (2 kg) total weight, frenched

In a bowl, whisk together the vinegar, wine, oil, and garlic. Cut the orange in half and squeeze the juice from both halves into the bowl. Cut the orange halves into thin slices and add to the marinade along with the mint, cilantro, and ¼ teaspoon each salt and pepper.

Place the lamb chops in a large lock-top plastic bag, pour in the marinade, and seal the bag. Marinate in the fridge for at least 1 hour or up to 24 hours.

Prepare a medium-hot fire in a charcoal or gas grill.

Remove the lamb chops from the bag and pour the marinade into a small saucepan. Grill the chops, turning once, for 3 minutes per side for medium-rare. (I like them a little more cooked, about 4 minutes per side.)

Meanwhile, place the saucepan holding the marinade over high heat and bring to a boil. Reduce the heat to medium-low and simmer for 4 minutes to create a sauce. Pour the sauce into a serving bowl.

Serve the lamb chops right away and pass the sauce at the table.

Serves 4–6

the kids' steaks

Grilling is the most common way to cook a steak. But I live in a New York City apartment, and cooking steaks on an indoor grill pan is one of my least favorite things to do. The apartment gets smoky, which sets off the smoke alarm. That means that the windows are thrown open, the kitchen exhaust fan is switched on, and, worst of all, my apartment smells like grilled steak for days! But my children love steak, so I have perfected a way to cook it without all the noise, smell, and smoke. I marinate small boneless rib-eye steaks and then cook them in a low oven for five hours. The meat comes out delicious and as soft as butter, which makes it easy for the kids to eat. Although I call these "kids' steaks," adults are crazy for them, too. I usually marinate them in the fridge overnight and then pop them into the oven the next afternoon, so they're ready to eat by dinnertime, but you can skip the overnight marinating.

6	small boneless rib-eye steaks, about 3 lb (1.5 kg) total weight and ¾ inch (2 cm) thick
	Kosher salt and freshly ground pepper
3	tablespoons tomato ketchup or tomato paste
3	tablespoons soy sauce
2	tablespoons balsamic vinegar
1	tablespoon Worcestershire sauce
1	tablespoon *silan* (date syrup) or pure raw honey
1	teaspoon dried oregano

Place the steaks in a single layer in 1 large or 2 medium rectangular baking dishes. Season them generously with salt and pepper. In a small bowl, whisk together the soy sauce, ketchup, vinegar, Worcestershire, *silan*, oregano, and 3 tablespoons water until thoroughly blended. Pour the mixture over the steaks, dividing it evenly if using 2 baking dishes. You can cook the steaks right away or you can cover the dish(es) and marinate them in the fridge for up to 24 hours.

Preheat the oven to 275°F (135°C).

Cover the baking dish(es) with aluminum foil, place in the oven, and cook for 4 hours. Remove from the oven, turn the steaks over, and raise the oven temperature to 325°F (165°C). Cook the steaks, uncovered, for 1 hour longer. The meat should be extremely tender and easy to cut with a fork, and the sauce should be deep brown and slightly thickened. Serve the steaks right away with the sauce spooned over the top.

Serves 6

veal roast with porcini, thyme & garlic rub

A veal roast is a great option when you are serving a crowd. This recipe uses dried porcini mushrooms, which can be found in most specialty-food shops; they add an incredible and distinct flavor. This dish is sophisticated enough for even your most cultured eaters, and it's yummy enough for youngsters, too.

3	tablespoons olive oil
1	boneless veal roast (top round or leg), about 5 lb (2.5 kg), tied
	Kosher salt and freshly ground pepper
5	yellow onions, about 2 lb (1 kg) total weight, thinly sliced
1	cup (1 oz/30 g) dried porcini mushrooms
4	cloves garlic
	Leaves from 12 fresh thyme sprigs
¼	cup (2 fl oz/60 ml) balsamic vinegar
1	cup (8 fl oz/250 ml) dry white wine

Preheat the oven to 375°F (190°C).

In a roasting pan large enough to hold the veal roast, heat the oil over medium-high heat. Season the roast on all sides with ½ teaspoon salt and ¼ teaspoon pepper. Add to the pan and brown for about 5 minutes per side. Transfer to a large plate. Add the onions to the pan and cook, stirring occasionally, until lightly browned, about 10 minutes.

Meanwhile, in a food processor, combine the mushrooms, garlic, and thyme and pulse until a paste forms. Use your hands to rub the paste all over the veal, then place the roast in the pan on top of the onions. Pour the vinegar and wine over the veal and bring to a boil over medium-high heat.

Cover the pan with aluminum foil, transfer to the oven, cook, turning the veal over once halfway through the cooking, for about 2 hours. The veal is ready when it can be easily pierced with a fork. Use tongs to carefully transfer the veal to a cutting board and let rest for about 10 minutes.

If serving right away, snip the strings, then cut the veal against the grain into slices ¼ inch (6 mm) thick. Arrange the slices on a large warmed platter. Reheat the sauce in the roasting pan on the stove top and spoon over the slices.

If serving later, let the veal cool, then wrap in foil and refrigerate overnight or up to 3 days to make slicing easier. Transfer the sauce to an airtight container and store in the fridge. Slice the meat as directed then reheat the veal and sauce in a 300°F (150°C) oven for 30–40 minutes.

Serves 8–12

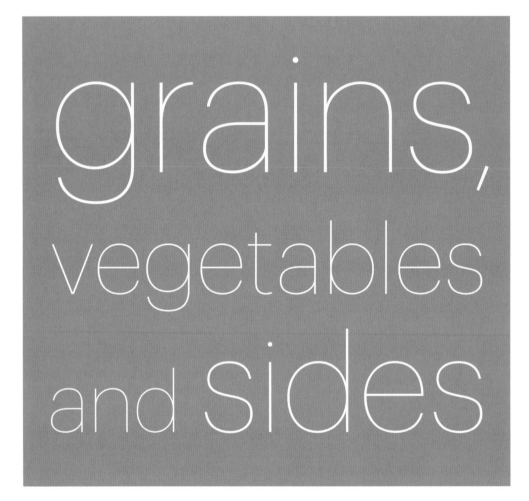

grains,
vegetables
and sides

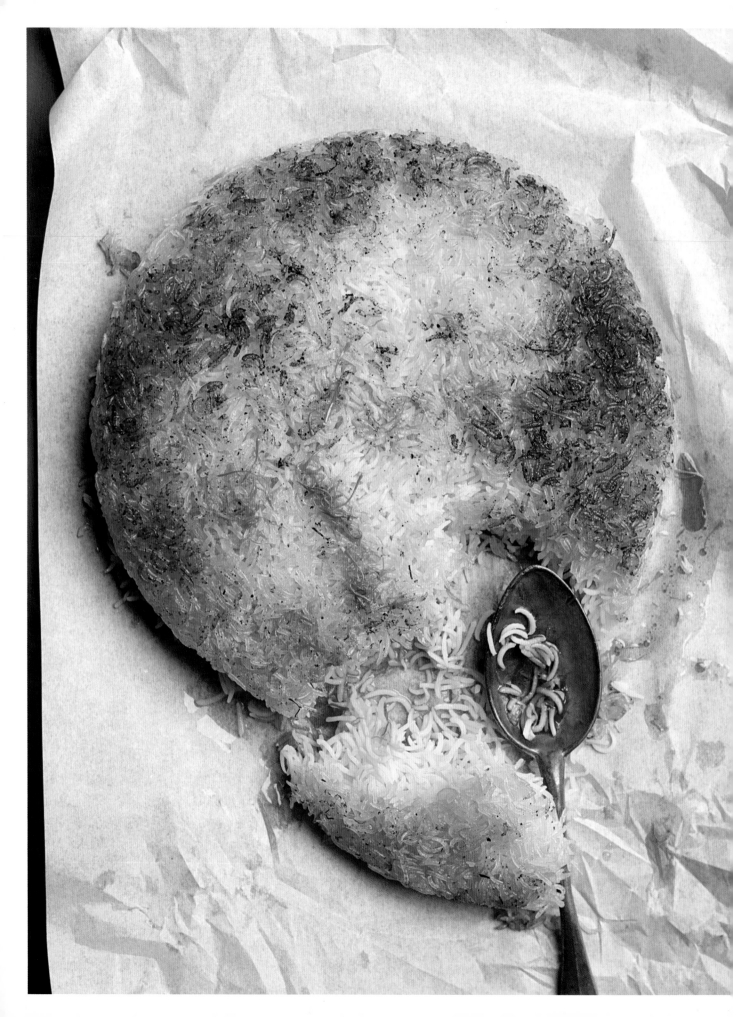

crispy rice cake with saffron crust

Who doesn't love crispy rice? This is a wonderful side dish to make year-round—crunchy, light, and flavorful. Serve with Savoy Slaw with Lemongrass & Lime Dressing (page 93) or alongside your favorite main dish. I cover the rice with a few paper towels as it cooks to absorb excess moisture, which helps to create a golden crust on the bottom of the rice.

2	cups (14 oz/440 g) basmati rice, well rinsed
	Kosher salt
3	tablespoons corn oil or rice bran oil
4	saffron threads, crushed between your fingertips
1	heaping teaspoon sweet paprika

In a large saucepan, bring 4 cups (32 fl oz/1 l) water to a rapid boil over high heat. Stir in the rice and 1 teaspoon salt. Reduce the heat to medium-low, cover, and cook for about 9 minutes. You don't want the rice to be fully cooked or the water to be completely absorbed. It should be only halfway there. Spoon the rice into a fine-mesh sieve placed over a bowl and let it stand until all of the liquid has drained.

Meanwhile, heat a large sauté pan over medium-high heat. Pour in the oil and use a wooden spoon to swirl the saffron and paprika into the oil. When the oil starts to sizzle, carefully spoon in the rice, pressing it into the bottom of the pan to form a sort of "rice cake." Reduce the heat to medium, place a few paper towels over the rice, and cover the pan. Cook until the rice cake is nicely browned and crisp, 15–20 minutes. Using a spatula, lift the cake occasionally to make sure the rice isn't burning. When the cake is ready, uncover and let cool for a few minutes.

Remove the paper towels. Carefully invert a large plate over the top of the pan, invert the plate and pan together, and then lift off the pan. Serve right away. The rice cake can also be made up to one hour ahead and kept covered at room temperature. Just before serving, reheat in a 300°F (150°C) oven.

Serves 10

red & white quinoa with mango & soy-peanut sauce

I like to combine red and white (aka golden) quinoa because of their different textures. The white quinoa is soft and glossy, and the red is crunchier and grainy. With the sweetness from the mango, the crunch from the sunflower seeds, and the burst of flavor from the soy-peanut sauce, this dish is off-the-charts delicious and takes just minutes to throw together.

½	cup (4 oz/125 g) red quinoa, well rinsed
½	cup (4 oz/125 g) white quinoa, well rinsed
	Kosher salt
1	mango
3	tablespoons extra-virgin olive oil
3	tablespoons soy sauce
1	tablespoon creamy peanut butter
1–2	tablespoons firmly packed dark brown sugar (depending on how sweet you like it)
3	tablespoons white vinegar
5	scallions, white and pale green parts only, minced
¼	cup (1 oz/30 g) salted, roasted sunflower seeds
2	tablespoons roasted sesame seeds
¼	cup (1½ oz/45 g) pomegranate seeds

In a saucepan, bring 1½ cups (12 fl oz/375 ml) water to a boil over high heat. Stir in the quinoa, and a pinch of salt. Reduce the heat to low, cover, and cook until all the water is absorbed, about 20 minutes. Uncover and let cool for about 5 minutes.

Meanwhile, peel and pit the mango and cut the flesh into small pieces, about the size of blueberries. In a small bowl, whisk together the oil, soy sauce, peanut butter, brown sugar, and vinegar until well blended.

In a bowl, combine the quinoa, mango, scallions, and sunflower seeds. Pour the dressing over the top and toss well. Garnish with the sesame seeds and pomegranate seeds. The quinoa will keep in an airtight container in the fridge for up to 3 days.

Serves 4–6

"bowl of crack" quinoa

Quinoa is all the rage. It's funny the way certain foods become popular, isn't it? Well, these little tiny grains have also become my latest obsession. But if you ask me, they must be prepared properly, and I have one simple but strict rule: Quinoa should never appear as the base of a dish. Instead, it should be distributed throughout the dish. I came up with this recipe one night, and at dinner, my husband said, "Pass over that bowl of crack!" That's what we've called it ever since. I use dill, cilantro, and flat-leaf parsley, but feel free to use any fresh herbs you like. I am definitely not a raisin person, but I found a bag of golden raisins that evening, and now they are an indispensable ingredient of the dish—mild and sweet, they look like little golden gems amid the quinoa grains.

1	cup (8 oz/250 g) white quinoa, well rinsed
	Kosher salt and freshly ground pepper
2	cups (5 oz/155 g) shredded kale
1	large bunch fresh dill
1	large bunch fresh cilantro
1	large bunch fresh flat-leaf parsley
	Juice of 1 lemon
	Juice of 2 limes
¼	cup (2 fl oz/60 ml) extra-virgin olive oil
3	tablespoons rice vinegar
1	handful of toasted pine nuts, pistachios, or chopped almonds
1	handful of golden raisins

In a saucepan, bring 2 cups (16 fl oz/500 ml) water to a boil over high heat. Stir in the quinoa and a pinch of salt. Reduce the heat to low, cover, and cook until all the water is absorbed, about 20 minutes. Uncover and let cool for about 10 minutes, and then transfer the quinoa to a large bowl. Stir in the kale.

Use a chef's knife to chop the dill, cilantro, and parsley into teeny-tiny pieces (I use the stems, too). Doing this by hand is important because a food processor will make the herbs mushy. Throw the herbs into the bowl. Add the lemon juice, lime juice, oil, and vinegar and toss to mix well. Stir in the pine nuts and raisins and season well with salt and pepper. The quinoa will keep in an airtight container in the fridge for up to 3 days.

Serves 4–6

crispy shaved brussels sprouts

This recipe is a good example of simplicity at its best. Shaving the brussels sprouts just means slicing them extremely thinly, but it always amazes me that by changing the texture and shape of the vegetable, everything else seems to change, too. After roasting them, the sprouts are crunchy and salty, and will almost melt in your mouth. I never make enough of this dish!

2	lb (1 kg) brussels sprouts
4	small scallions, white and pale green parts only
⅓	cup (3 fl oz/80 ml) extra-virgin olive oil
½	teaspoon dried thyme or leaves from 4 fresh thyme sprigs
	Kosher salt and freshly ground pepper

Preheat the oven to 350°F (180°C).

Use a very sharp knife to trim off the base of each brussels sprout. Cut each sprout in half lengthwise, then cut each half crosswise into extremely thin slices, almost like shavings. Place in a rectangular baking dish.

Slice the scallions as thinly as possible, add to the brussels sprouts, and toss to mix. Drizzle with the oil and sprinkle with the thyme, ½ teaspoon salt, and ¼ teaspoon pepper. Toss well and spread out in an even layer.

Roast until crisp and golden, 30–40 minutes. The sprouts are best served straight from the oven.

Serves 6

roasted zucchini with sage bread crumbs

I like a recipe that is simple, straightforward, and tasty. I like a recipe that I can understand the first time I read it. This one meets all my criteria. There's not much to think about, but it will keep you wanting more. Roasted zucchini slices are topped with savory, toasty herbed bread crumbs. You can't get it wrong.

3	large zucchini, cut into rounds ¼ inch (6 mm) thick
¾	cup (3 oz/90 g) dried bread crumbs
4	fresh sage leaves
½	teaspoon garlic powder
¼	teaspoon ground ginger
¼	teaspoon ground nutmeg
1	handful of pine nuts (optional)
3	tablespoons extra-virgin olive oil or 2 tablespoons unsalted butter, melted, plus oil or melted butter for brushing
	Kosher salt and freshly ground pepper

Preheat the oven to 400°F (200°C). Line a baking sheet with parchment paper.

Spread the zucchini in an even layer on the prepared baking sheet. Cover with aluminum foil, place in the oven, and cook for 10 minutes.

Meanwhile, in a mini food processor, combine the bread crumbs, sage leaves, garlic powder, ginger, nutmeg, pine nuts (if using), oil, and ¼ teaspoon each salt and pepper. Process until the mixture is crumbly, like sand.

Remove the zucchini from the oven and reduce the oven temperature to 350°F (180°C). Brush the slices with a little oil and sprinkle evenly with the crumb topping. Roast until the crumbs are golden brown, about 15 minutes longer.

Serve right away or at room temperature. If preparing in advance, let the zucchini cool completely, then cover with plastic wrap and store in the fridge for up to 1 day. Reheat in a 300°F (150°C) oven for 30 minutes.

Serves 6-8

crispy smashed za'atar potatoes

It seems that my cooking students are always looking for an easy side dish that will be a big crowd-pleaser. This one is definitely a winner. The key is to use small potatoes, like ruby or golden marble potatoes. I parboil them in simmering water, smash them with the back of a large fork or with a potato masher, and then roast them in an extra-hot oven until golden and crisp. These potatoes are delectable.

2½	lb (1.25 kg) marble potatoes or other small potatoes
	Kosher salt and freshly ground pepper
¼	cup (2 fl oz/60 ml) extra-virgin olive oil
3–4	tablespoons za'atar

Preheat the oven to 425°F (220°C).

Place the potatoes in a large pot and add cold water to cover. Bring to a boil over high heat and stir in 1 tablespoon salt. Cover, reduce the heat to medium, and cook until fork-tender, about 10 minutes depending on size.

Drain the potatoes and spread in a single layer on a baking sheet. Use a large fork or a potato masher to smash them slightly. You just want to break them up a bit. Drizzle the oil over the top and season generously with salt and pepper. Taste and adjust the seasoning.

Roast until the potatoes are golden and crisp, about 10 minutes. As soon as they come out of the oven, sprinkle generously with the za'atar to taste and serve right away.

Serves 6–8

kim's quick latkes

Making latkes can be messy, time-consuming, and exhausting. But because there's nothing like eating a hot homemade latke, every year I succumb to the pressure and make a big batch. In the past, I would spend hours grating potatoes, and the gratings would invariably end up all over the place: in my hair, on the lampshades, on the floor. I knew there must be another way. The answer was the food processor. Now, I put all the ingredients into my processor fitted with the metal blade, pulse and process briefly, and I am done. It is a fuss-free, super-easy solution to a long-standing problem, and the results are mouthwatering. The latkes are crisp on the outside, soft on the inside, and freeze beautifully. If you like, sprinkle the latkes with truffle salt just as they come out of the frying pan—a divine addition. (If you plan to do this, reduce the kosher salt to ½ teaspoon.)

5	Yukon gold or red potatoes, about 2 lb (1 kg) total weight, peeled and cut into large chunks
1	large yellow onion, cut into large chunks
2	large eggs
⅓	cup (2 oz/60 g) all-purpose flour
1	teaspoon baking powder
	Kosher salt and freshly ground pepper
½	cup (4 fl oz/125 ml) rice bran oil or canola oil

Preheat the oven to 400°F (200°C).

In a food processor, combine the potatoes, onion, and eggs and process with quick on-off pulses until the potatoes and onion are chopped into small pieces, about 30 seconds. Add the flour, baking powder, 1 teaspoon salt, and ¼ teaspoon pepper and process until the ingredients are well combined, a couple of seconds longer.

In a large frying pan, heat the oil over medium-high heat. Using an ice-cream scoop (you know I like to make sure they are all the same size!), scoop up the potato mixture, drop into the hot oil, and flatten with a spatula or fork to about ¼–½ inch (6–12 mm) thick. Cook only 4 latkes at a time so you don't crowd the pan. Once the edges are browned, carefully flip the latkes over and cook until the underside is crisp and golden, about 2 minutes per side. Transfer the latkes to paper towels to drain. Repeat with the remaining potato mixture. You can serve them right away, but I like to arrange them in a single layer on a baking sheet and put them in the oven for 3–5 minutes to give them a final crisping.

To freeze the latkes, let them cool completely, then freeze them in a single layer in large lock-top plastic freezer bags for up to 1 month. To serve, thaw in the refrigerator overnight and reheat in a 375°F (190°C) oven until piping hot, 8–10 minutes.

Makes about 24 latkes

roasted eggplant & red onion with yogurt dipping sauce

This is one of my all-time favorite recipes. I always have eggplant on hand and whip this up sometimes just to stuff into a pita for lunch. The combination of eggplant and red onion brings out some superb flavors, and the cool yogurt sauce adds an extra burst of tanginess. I like the addition of pomegranate seeds, though you can make the sauce without them.

1	eggplant, cut crosswise into slices ¼ inch (6 mm) thick
1	small red onion, cut into wedges or thinly sliced
¼	cup (2 fl oz/60 ml) extra-virgin olive oil
	Kosher salt and freshly ground pepper
	Best-Ever Yogurt Dipping Sauce (page 14)

Preheat the oven to 425°F (220°C). Line a baking sheet with parchment paper.

In a large bowl, combine the eggplant, onion, and oil and season with 1 teaspoon salt and ½ teaspoon pepper. Toss well, transfer to the prepared baking sheet, and spread in an even layer.

Roast for 15 minutes, then stir the vegetables and continue to roast until softened and golden, about 10 minutes longer.

Ready the dipping sauce as directed, reserving some of the pomegranate seeds. Arrange the roasted vegetables on a serving platter, scatter the reserved pomegranate seeds over the top, and serve the dipping sauce alongside. Serve warm or at room temperature.

Serves 6–8

roasted radicchio, endive & fennel

What comes to mind when you hear "roasted vegetables"? Potatoes? Eggplant? Squash? These are often the same vegetables we turn to regularly. It always irks me that sometimes the best choices are overlooked. This is one of my most popular winter vegetable dishes. The colors of the deep red radicchio and bright green endives are gorgeous, and the flavor of the fennel mellows when roasted, making this dish easy to serve alongside nearly any main course.

2	small heads radicchio, quartered through the stem end
4	heads Belgian endive, about 1 lb (500 g) total weight, halved lengthwise
1	fennel bulb, trimmed, cored, and sliced
2	tablespoons extra-virgin olive oil
1	tablespoon melted coconut oil
1	tablespoon balsamic vinegar
1	heaping tablespoon sugar
	Kosher salt and freshly ground pepper

Preheat the oven to 375°F (190°C). Line a baking sheet with parchment paper.

In a large bowl, combine the radicchio, endive, and fennel. Add the oils, vinegar, sugar, ½ teaspoon salt, and ¼ teaspoon pepper. Toss well, transfer to the prepared baking sheet, and spread out in an even layer.

Roast for 30 minutes, then raise the oven temperature to 450°F (230°C) and roast until the vegetables are crisping slightly on the edges, about 5 minutes longer. Serve warm or at room temperature.

Serves 6–8

spicy ginger-carrot slaw with rice

When you're short on time and want a quick, light meal, rice bowls are a great way to go. Simply steam white or brown rice, scoop it into bowls, arrange cooked sliced chicken, beef, fish, or tofu over the rice, and then spoon this spicy, fresh-tasting, flavorful slaw on top—dinner in no time, served with a spoon! This recipe is also a good template for how to use up leftover rice and/or whatever protein you may have in the fridge.

3	Kirby (pickling) cucumbers, halved lengthwise and very thinly sliced crosswise
3	cups (15 oz/470 g) peeled and shredded or julienned carrots
1	cup (3 oz/90 g) shredded green cabbage
½	red onion, chopped
3	tablespoons chopped fresh cilantro
3	tablespoons chopped fresh flat-leaf parsley
1	3-inch (7.5-cm) piece fresh ginger, peeled and diced
¼	cup (2 fl oz/60 ml) rice vinegar
	Juice of 2 limes
2	tablespoons sugar
1	tablespoon toasted sesame oil
¼	cup (1⅓ oz/40 g) sesame seeds
5	cups (25 oz/780 g) hot steamed rice
	Cooked chicken, beef, fish, or tofu for serving

In a large bowl, toss together the cucumbers, carrots, cabbage, onion, cilantro, and parsley.

In a food processor, combine the ginger, vinegar, lime juice, sugar, and oil and process until a paste forms, about 30 seconds. Pour the dressing over the slaw and use your hands to toss together thoroughly. Add the sesame seeds and toss to mix.

The slaw can be prepared just before serving or up to 3 hours in advance and refrigerated. To serve, divide the rice evenly among individual bowls and top with chicken or other protein and then the slaw. Serve right away.

Serves 6-8

spaghetti with fresh 5-minute tomato sauce

Summer in New York City can be brutally hot—too hot to cook. I am the first to admit it. There's no way I am going to stand over my stove cooking, no matter how strong my air-conditioning is blowing. After a long, hot day, all I want to do is sit on the couch and eat a satisfying, fuss-free, home-cooked dinner out of a bowl. This simple pasta dish is the answer. The only cooking you have to do is boil the pasta. This is my version of a fast, homemade, perfect-for-the-summer pasta sauce. All you need are four ingredients—ripe tomatoes, a garlic clove, pine nuts, and fresh basil—and about 5 minutes. That's my kind of dinner. After I spoon the sauce over the hot pasta, I like to drizzle a little extra-virgin olive oil over the sauce. At the table, I set out freshly grated Parmesan, though ricotta or fresh mozzarella is good too, and red pepper flakes.

3–4	very ripe tomatoes, quartered
1	clove garlic
¼	cup (1¼ oz/40 g) pine nuts (toasted or raw)
	Kosher salt and freshly ground pepper
1	package (1 lb/500 g) spaghetti
4–5	fresh basil leaves for garnish

In a food processor, combine the tomatoes, garlic, and pine nuts and process until a light, creamy sauce forms. Season with salt and pepper.

Bring a pot of salted water to a boil over high heat. Cook the spaghetti according to the package directions. Drain and transfer to a large bowl. Spoon the sauce over the hot pasta, garnish with the basil, and serve right away.

The sauce will keep in a tightly capped glass jar in the fridge for up to 1 week.

Serves 6

favorite
sweets

dark chocolate bark with rose petals, pistachios & walnuts

I am always looking for a showstopping dessert that will wow company, and this recipe does just that. A sheet of silky chocolate bark is sprinkled with bright green crushed pistachios, light pink rose petals, and crunchy walnuts, then broken into pieces. To crush the pistachios, place them in a plastic bag, seal tightly, and strike with a wooden mallet or a rolling pin. This chocolate bark is beautiful, tasty, and fun to eat. And believe it or not, it's also easy! Once you get the hang of making your own chocolate bark, you will love personalizing it with your favorite toppings. You can prepare the bark ahead of time and store in the fridge until ready to serve.

9	oz (280 g) dark chocolate (bars, chips, or chunks)
½	cup (2 oz/60 g) crushed unsalted pistachios
2	tablespoons crushed dried rose petals
¼	cup (1 oz/30 g) chopped walnuts

Line a baking sheet with parchment paper.

If you are using chocolate bars, break them into small pieces. Put the chocolate in the top pan of a double boiler over (not touching) simmering water and heat, stirring often with a heat-resistant spatula, until melted and smooth. Let cool for 3 minutes.

Pour the chocolate onto the prepared baking sheet and use a spatula to smooth into an even layer. Sprinkle the pistachios, rose petals, and walnuts evenly over the chocolate. Place the baking sheet on a level shelf in the fridge until the bark is completely cooled and hardened, about 2 hours. The bark can be covered and stored in the fridge for up to 2 weeks.

To serve, carefully peel the bark off the parchment paper, place it on a wooden board, and break it into pieces with a wooden mallet, or break it up with your hands. Place in a serving dish.

Serves 12

miniature peanut butter cups

These bite-sized, melt-in-your-mouth sensations require no baking and can be stored in the fridge for weeks. People are crazy for them. I found the original recipe in one of Nigella Lawson's cookbooks. She calls them Peanut Butter Squares, but over time I changed a few things and made them my own. They work particularly well as miniature treats because they are rich and creamy. But that's not to say that just one will ever be enough.

1	teaspoon coconut or canola oil
¼	cup (2 oz/60 g) firmly packed dark brown sugar
1⅓	cups (5½ oz/170 g) confectioners' sugar
5	tablespoons (2½ oz/75 g) unsalted butter, at room temperature
1	cup (10 oz/315 g) creamy or chunky peanut butter
3	oz (90 g) dark or milk chocolate, chopped
1½	cups (9 oz/280 g) semisweet chocolate chips

Grease a 9-inch (23-cm) square baking pan with the oil.

In a stand mixer fitted with the paddle attachment, beat together the sugars, 4 tablespoons (2 oz/60 g) of the butter, and the peanut butter on high speed until the ingredients are well combined and the mixture is sandy, about 3 minutes. Transfer the mixture to the prepared baking pan and use your hands to press it evenly onto the bottom. You might find that dampening your hands will make it easier to spread the mixture evenly.

Put all of the chocolate in the top pan of a double boiler over (not touching) simmering water and heat, stirring often with a heat-resistant spatula, until melted and smooth. Let cool for 3 minutes.

Use the spatula to spread the chocolate mixture evenly over the peanut butter mixture. Place in the fridge until set, about 3 hours. It can be covered and stored in the fridge for up to 1 week.

At this point, you have two choices: You can use a knife to cut the mixture into small squares, or you can use cookie cutters to cut out fun shapes. I like to use a small round cookie cutter (about the size of a quarter). Before using cutters, it helps to let the mixture stand at room temperature for about 30 minutes so it softens just a bit.

When I have removed the shapes from the pan, I smush together whatever edges are left in the pan to form another layer. I let the layer sit in the fridge until it hardens, and then I use the cutters to cut out more shapes. I repeat this process until nothing is left. I hate to see any of this gorgeous peanut butter perfection go to waste.

Makes about 40 round mini cups

the perfect stormy cake

This is just the type of dessert you want to have on hand on a rainy, glum day—paired with a steaming cup of coffee, of course—thus, its name. Unlike a typical coffee cake, which is all nuts and cake, I've added cocoa powder, which lends an element of surprise and richness. You can make the cake in advance and freeze it, then pull it out on one of those stormy days. This recipe is based on Norene Gilletz's Best Coffee Cake from *The Food Processor Bible*.

Nonstick cooking spray for pan

For the Topping and Filling

¾	cup (3 oz/90 g) pecans or almonds
½	cup (3½ oz/105 g) firmly packed dark brown sugar
2	teaspoons ground cinnamon
1	tablespoon unsweetened cocoa powder
1	cup (6 oz/185 g) chocolate chips

For the Batter

6	tablespoons (3 oz/90 g) cold unsalted butter
1	cup (8 oz/250 g) granulated sugar
2	large eggs
1	teaspoon vanilla extract
1	teaspoon baking soda
1	cup (8 oz/250 g) sour cream or plain yogurt
1⅓	cups (7 oz/220 g) all-purpose flour
1½	teaspoons baking powder

Preheat the oven to 350°F (180°C). Lightly spray a 9-inch (23-cm) round cake pan with nonstick cooking spray.

To make the topping and filling, in a food processor, combine the pecans, brown sugar, cinnamon, and cocoa powder and process with 6–8 quick on-off pulses until the nuts are coarsely chopped. Transfer to a bowl and stir in the chocolate chips. Wipe out the processor bowl with a paper towel.

To make the batter, in the processor, combine the butter, granulated sugar, eggs, and vanilla and pulse for 2 minutes, stopping to scrape down the sides of the bowl as needed. Do not insert the pusher into the feed tube. In a small bowl, dissolve the baking soda in the sour cream. Add to the processor and pulse for 3 seconds. Add the flour and baking powder and pulse with 4 quick on-off pulses, just until the flour is blended into the batter. Do not overprocess, and stop to scrape down the bowl as needed.

Pour half of the batter into the prepared pan and sprinkle with half of the topping. Repeat with the remaining batter and topping.

Bake until a toothpick inserted into the center of the cake comes out clean, 40–45 minutes.

Let cool in the pan on a wire rack for 1 hour before serving. To freeze, invert onto a plate lined with plastic wrap then again onto a serving plate, being careful not to lose too much crumb topping. Wrap tightly in plastic wrap, place in a plastic freezer bag, and freeze for up to 1 month. Thaw at room temperature before serving.

Makes one 9-inch (23-cm) cake; serves 6–8

cinnamon-chocolate pound cake with greek yogurt

While I was growing up, I watched my mom bake a cake every Friday, and now I try to do the same thing. I love waking up to a great piece of cake with my Saturday morning coffee. Here is a golden pound cake made with creamy Greek yogurt, speckles of aromatic cinnamon, and melty chocolate chunks.

1	teaspoon coconut or corn oil
1⅓	cups (7 oz/220 g) all-purpose flour
1½	teaspoons baking powder
1	teaspoon baking soda
1	heaping teaspoon ground cinnamon
½	cup (4 oz/125 g) unsalted butter, at room temperature
1	cup (8 oz/250 g) sugar
2	large eggs
1	cup (8 oz/250 g) plain or vanilla Greek yogurt
1	cup (5 oz/150 g) dark chocolate chunks

Preheat the oven to 350°F (180°C). Grease a 9-inch (23-cm) springform pan with the oil.

In a bowl, stir together the flour, baking powder, baking soda, and cinnamon. Set aside.

In a stand mixer fitted with the paddle attachment, beat together the butter and sugar on high speed until smooth, about 3 minutes. Add the eggs and yogurt and beat until combined, about 2 minutes. On low speed, add the flour mixture and beat just until combined. Fold in the chocolate chunks. Pour the batter into the prepared pan.

Bake until a toothpick inserted into the center of the cake comes out clean, about 40 minutes. If it is not done, bake for 5 minutes longer.

Let cool in the pan on a wire rack for 1 hour before unclasping the pan sides and transferring the cake to a serving plate. Store the cake, covered and in a cool place, for up to 4 days.

Makes one 9-inch (23-cm) cake; serves 6–8

giant chocolate chip–oatmeal cookie

A very kid-friendly recipe, this dessert takes just 10 minutes to prepare and 15 minutes to bake in the oven. And you probably have all the ingredients at home. When I'm hosting a dinner party, I make the dough and press it into the tart pan early in the day and then I store it in the fridge until I'm ready to bake it. Then, 15 minutes before I want to serve dessert, I pop the pan into the oven. The freshly baked cookie aroma that fills my apartment is heavenly. I serve this giant cookie warm. Try it and you will thank me, and your guests will thank you! Serve the cookie with ice cream, fresh fruit, coffee, milk, or any way you like.

1	teaspoon coconut oil or canola oil
½	cup (4 oz/125 g) unsalted butter, at room temperature or ¼ cup (2 fl oz/60 ml) rice bran oil plus ¼ cup (2 fl oz/60 ml) melted coconut oil
½	cup (4 oz/125 g) granulated sugar
½	cup (3½ oz/105 g) firmly packed dark brown sugar
	Kosher salt
1	large egg
1	teaspoon vanilla extract
1½	cups (7½ oz/235 g) all-purpose flour
¼	cup (¾ oz/20 g) old-fashioned rolled oats
1	cup (6 oz/185 g) semisweet chocolate chips (I mix regular and mini)
¼	cup (1 oz/30 g) chopped pecans (optional)

Preheat the oven to 375°F (190°C). Use the 1 teaspoon oil to grease an 11-inch (28-cm) round tart pan with a removable bottom.

In a stand mixer fitted with the paddle attachment, beat together the butter, sugars, and ¼ teaspoon salt on high speed until creamy, about 3 minutes. Add the egg and vanilla and beat until creamy, about 2 minutes. Stir in the flour, oats, chocolate chips, and pecans (if using) just until combined. Do not overmix.

Use your fingers to spread the dough evenly into the prepared pan. It might seem like there isn't enough dough to cover the bottom of the pan, but dampen your hands with cold water and use your fingers to stretch the dough out. You will have more than enough.

Bake until the edges of the cookie are golden, about 15 minutes. Let cool in the pan on a wire rack for 30 minutes, then remove the cookie from the pan. Slice like a pizza to serve.

Makes one 11-inch (28-cm) cookie; serves 8–10

chocolate-drizzled coconut macaroons

These days, French *macarons* are getting all the attention, and they totally deserve it because of their gorgeous colors, inventive flavors, and serious technique. But the average person is not going to attempt to whip up those French delicacies. They take too much time and skill. But whatever happened to the old-fashioned version that's crunchy on the outside and soft and cloudy on the inside? I'm not talking about the hard-as-rock, artificially flavored Passover ones. I'm referring to the old-school coconutty, flaky, dreamy ones—the ones you can make at home and make your place smell like heaven, the ones that make you feel like crying for joy when you take the first bite. (Okay, maybe that's only me.) Here's an easy, straightforward recipe for these beauties. They will keep in an airtight container at room temperature for up to 1 week or in the freezer for up to 1 month.

2	14-oz (40-g) packages sweetened coconut flakes (about 10 cups)
3	tablespoons sweetened condensed milk
5	large egg whites, at room temperature
¼	teaspoon cream of tartar
¼	cup (2 oz/60 g) sugar
1	teaspoon vanilla extract
6	oz (185 g) of your favorite chocolate, melted

Preheat the oven to 325°F (165°C).

Spread the coconut in an even layer on an unlined baking sheet. Toast in the oven until fragrant, about 10 minutes. Let cool, stir the milk in, and use your hands to combine well. Do not turn off the oven.

In a stand mixer fitted with the whisk attachment, beat together the egg whites and cream of tartar on medium speed until frothy, about 4 minutes. Add the sugar, increase the speed to medium-high, and beat until the mixture is opaque and soft peaks form, about 3 minutes. Add the vanilla, increase the speed to high, and beat until stiff, glossy peaks form, about 2 minutes. Use a spatula to fold in the coconut mixture.

Line 2 baking sheets with parchment paper. Using a ¼-cup (2–fl oz/60-ml) measuring cup, drop the mixture onto the prepared baking sheets, spacing the cookies about 2 inches (5 cm) apart. They should form tall mounds, rather than wide ones. Bake, one sheet at a time, until the tops and bottoms of the cookies are browned and the insides are still a little soft, 15–20 minutes; they will harden as they cool. Let cool completely on the pans on wire racks. Turn the oven off. After it has cooled down a bit, return the cookies to the oven and leave them there overnight. The next day, peel the macaroons off the parchment and drizzle with the melted chocolate.

Makes about 24 macaroons

crunchy-chewy-nutty "health" cookies

I've never claimed to be a health-food cook. I definitely try to cook using fresh, seasonal ingredients, but I'm not one to turn away a recipe because it includes a stick of butter. I like food that tastes good, and if it happens to be good for me, too, that's just a bonus. This recipe was given to me by my cousin in Israel, who is an amazing cook. It's a sticky, gooey cookie full of almonds, sesame seeds, pumpkin seeds, and sunflower seeds. It takes just seconds to throw together, and the baking time is about 20 minutes. The cookies are crunchy and light tasting and just great to have on hand. But what I like the most about these cookies is the reaction they always get. "You made those? No way!" Everyone always assumes they are store-bought. And as for the health factor, in my family, when a recipe calls for seeds and nuts, it is automatically labeled "healthy." We just pretend that the sugar isn't in it. Maybe we should call them "healthy enough?"

1½	cups (7 oz/215 g) slivered blanched almonds
1¼	cups (6 oz/185 g) sesame seeds
1	cup (4 oz/125 g) shelled pumpkin seeds
1	cup (4 oz/125 g) unsalted sunflower seeds
3	large egg whites
¾	cup (6 oz/185 g) firmly packed light brown sugar

Preheat the oven to 325°F (165°C). Line 2 baking sheets with parchment paper.

In a large bowl, stir together the almonds and seeds. In a small bowl, whisk together the egg whites and brown sugar. Add the egg white mixture to the almond mixture and use your hands to combine.

Using a tablespoon or a mini ice-cream scoop, drop heaping tablespoons of the mixture onto the prepared baking sheets, spacing the cookies about 1 inch (2.5 cm) apart. Flatten slightly with your fingertips.

Bake both baking sheets, rotating the pans back to front every 10 minutes, until the cookies are golden brown, 20–30 minutes. They may still be a little soft but will harden after they cool on the pans on wire racks for 20 minutes. The cookies will keep in an airtight container at room temperature for up to 2 weeks.

Makes about 30 cookies

pecan & lemon zest thumbprint cookies

When it comes to baking, a lot of my cooking students tell me they are too scared to go outside of their comfort zone. As a result, many people stick to their tried-and-true family recipes, like chocolate chip cookies or brownies. I am all about tried-and-true, but once in a while, it is a good idea to bake something new, something that might seem a little less straightforward than the usual, but that offers a great homey taste. The old-fashioned thumbprint cookie is the answer. These are simple to make and take just a few minutes more than chocolate chip cookies. I like to keep them light but nutty by using finely chopped pecans. My secret ingredient is grated lemon zest, which nicely tempers both the richness and the sweetness. These cookies freeze really well. Just place them in a single layer in lock-top plastic freezer bags and freeze for up to 1 month.

¾	cup (3 oz/90 g) pecans, walnuts, or almonds
1½	cups (8 oz/245 g) all-purpose flour
½	cup (4 oz/125 g) unsalted butter, at room temperature
½	cup (2 oz/60 g) confectioners' sugar
	Kosher salt
1	large egg
	Finely grated zest of 1 lemon
½	cup (5 oz/155 g) jam or preserves

In a food processor, combine the pecans and ¼ cup (1½ oz/45 g) of the flour and pulse until the nuts are very finely chopped. Set aside.

In a stand mixer fitted with the paddle attachment, combine the remaining 1¼ cups (6½ oz/200 g) flour, the butter, the confectioners' sugar, and a pinch of salt and beat on medium speed to combine. Add the pecan mixture, egg, and lemon zest, increase the speed to high, and beat just until the ingredients are combined and a dough forms, about 2 minutes. Cover and refrigerate the dough for about 30 minutes.

Preheat the oven to 350°F (180°C). Line a baking sheet with parchment paper.

Break off pieces of dough, shape into 1-inch (2.5-cm) balls, and place on the prepared baking sheet, spacing them about 2 inches (5 cm) apart. Flatten with fingertips. Use your thumb or the end of a wooden spoon handle to make an indentation in the center of each cookie. Fill with a little dollop of jam. Don't use too much jam, or it will overflow during baking.

Bake until the cookies are golden, 18–22 minutes. Let cool on a wire rack for 15 minutes and serve warm. The cookies will keep in an airtight container at room temperature for up to 5 days.

Makes about 24 cookies

deconstructed s'mores

I wish that I could take credit for this idea, but I can't. This is the most perfect, delicious, quirky dessert. I love the new bite-sized approach to food, and I think it's really neat to go to a party and be handed tuna tartare in a spoon or gazpacho in a shot glass. So why not attempt it with desserts? My cousin Natou had me over for dessert and gave me a deconstructed lemon meringue pie, nestled in its own mini glass jar with matching lid. It was to die for. Of course, it's one thing if the dessert looks unbelievably scrumptious, but it's a whole other ball game when it tastes as good as it looks. Well, these babies do. Here is my adaptation of a campfire favorite. I've used Greek yogurt and chocolate, but you can use store-bought chocolate pudding instead. And if chocolate is not your thing, try vanilla or coconut pudding, or even lemon or lime curd. Have fun with it.

3   **oz (90 g) of your favorite chocolate, chopped, or ½ cup (3 oz/90 g) chocolate chips**

3   **cups (24 oz/750 g) plain or vanilla Greek yogurt**

¾   **cup (2¼ oz/70 g) Perfect Graham Cracker Crumbs (page 36)**

     About ¾ cup (2 oz/60 g) marshmallow fluff

Have ready 12 individual dishes, such as mini glass jars, shot glasses, or small bowls, 3–4 fl oz (90–125 ml) each. I find these at a local dollar store.

Put the chocolate in the top pan of a double boiler over (not touching) simmering water and heat, stirring often with a heat-resistant spatula, until melted and smooth. Let cool completely, then stir in the yogurt until well combined. Cover with plastic wrap and place in the fridge until ready to assemble.

To assemble, fill the individual dishes halfway with the chocolate yogurt, sprinkle each serving with 1 tablespoon graham cracker crumbs, and carefully top with about 1 tablespoon marshmallow fluff. Cover the dishes (if they don't come with lids, use plastic wrap) and refrigerate until ready to serve or for up to 2 days. If you like, just before serving, use a kitchen torch to toast the marshmallow fluff lightly.

Serves 12

hamantaschen with three fillings

I think I've tried every dough recipe for hamantaschen that exists. And this one is my hands-down favorite. The key to making hamantaschen that hold together in the oven—we've all seen those oozing, exploding ones—is to bake them when they are frozen. Yes! After forming the hamantaschen, I place them in the freezer for a minimum of 1 hour or up to 48 hours, and then I transfer them directly from the freezer to a preheated oven (after a quick brush of egg wash). This will leave you with perfectly shaped, mouthwatering hamantaschen. I guess the secret is out of the bag!

4	large eggs
1½	cups (12 oz/375 g) sugar
1	cup (8 fl oz/250 ml) rice bran or canola oil
1	tablespoon vanilla extract
	Finely grated zest of 1 lemon
6	cups (30 oz/940 g) all-purpose flour
2	tablespoons baking powder
	Kosher salt
	Fillings of choice (see opposite)

In a stand mixer fitted with the whisk attachment, beat the eggs on high speed until creamy, about 2 minutes. Add the sugar, oil, vanilla, and lemon zest and beat until well combined, about 2 minutes. Switch to the paddle attachment, reduce the speed to low, and beat in the flour, baking powder, and 1 teaspoon salt until a soft, nonsticky dough forms (or, fold in with a spatula).

Divide the dough into 5 equal balls and wrap separately in plastic wrap. Chill in the fridge for at least 1 hour or up to 48 hours. Remove from the fridge and let soften on the countertop for 10 minutes before rolling out the dough. You can also freeze the dough for up to 2 months; thaw overnight in the fridge.

Preheat the oven to 350°F (180°C). Line 4 baking sheets with parchment paper.

Place a ball of dough on a piece of parchment paper and roll out into a round ⅛ inch (3 mm) thick. Use an overturned glass or a cookie cutter to cut the dough into 4-inch (10-cm) rounds. Place the filling in the center of each round as directed. To shape each triangular hamantasch, fold the left side of the round toward the center and then fold the right side toward the center, overlapping the sides slightly at the top. Fold the bottom of the round up to complete the triangle, leaving a small opening that reveals the filling in the center.

Pinch the seams tightly to secure. Reroll the scraps, cut out more rounds, and shape as directed above. Repeat with the remaining dough and fillings. Place the hamantaschen on the prepared baking sheets, spacing them about 1 inch (2.5 cm) apart. Place the baking sheets in the freezer for a minimum of 1 hour or up to 48 hours, until ready to bake.

Bake 2 sheets at a time, rotating the sheets back to front midway during baking, until the hamantaschen are golden, 15–20 minutes. Let cool on the pans on wire racks for 15 minutes. Freeze in a single layer in lock-top plastic freezer bags for up to 1 month. Thaw at room temperature before serving.

Makes about 24 hamantaschen

There are no specific measurements for these fillings, so just eyeball the amount of each ingredient. You really can't make a mistake, I promise.

Rocky Road Filling

Chocolate pieces of your choice (Rolo, Hershey's Kisses, and M&M'S work well, too)

Mini marshmallows

Pretzels, broken into small pieces

Marshmallow fluff or melted marshmallows

In a small bowl, stir together chocolate pieces, marshmallows, and pretzels. Place 1 teaspoon filling in the center of each dough round. Fold the dough and bake as directed. Drizzle marshmallow fluff sparingly over the cooled hamantaschen.

Cookies & Cream Filling

Chocolate or peanut butter spread (something that will allow the cookie bits to stick to the dough)

Cookies of your choice, broken into small pieces

Chocolate of your choice, melted

Place a small dollop of the spread in the center of each dough round. Top with about 1 teaspoon cookie pieces. Fold the dough and bake as directed. Drizzle melted chocolate over the cooled hamantaschen.

Ferrero Rocher Filling

Ferrero Rocher chocolates, broken into tiny pieces, or blanched and roasted hazelnuts; chocolate of choice, melted; and Nutella

Unsweetened cocoa powder for dusting

If using Ferrero Rocher chocolates, place a few pieces in the center of each dough round. Alternatively, dip hazelnuts in the melted chocolate and let dry on a plate. Place 1 teaspoon Nutella in the center of each dough round and place a chocolate-coated hazelnut in the center of the Nutella. Fold the dough and bake as directed. Dust the cooled hamantaschen with cocoa powder.

almond granita

Almond granita sounds fancy and complicated, but it is actually easy and mind-blowingly delicious. Granita is a semifrozen dessert with a granular texture that can be made in various flavors. I know that almond might not be the first flavor that comes to mind, but I love the unique, rich taste, and its lightness takes you by surprise. It's a refreshing way to end a meal. You don't need any equipment other than a rectangular dish and a fork. If you want to spice things up, add ½ cup (4 fl oz/ 125 ml) booze to the mix (rum or flavored vodka works well). You can make this dessert weeks in advance and have it waiting in your freezer for the perfect occasion (you know, one of those out-of-the-blue, sunny days when you decide to throw a last-minute barbecue or have friends over for drinks). Serve the granita in bowls or, to kitsch things up, in wine-glasses, martini glasses, or miniature jars. You can even portion it into serving dishes ahead of time, so they are frosty and ready to go.

¼	cup (2 oz/60 g) almond paste
⅓	cup (3 oz/90 g) sugar
½	cup (2½ oz/75 g) slivered blanched almonds, toasted
1¼	cups (10 fl oz/310 ml) whole milk, soy milk, or nondairy creamer
½	teaspoon almond extract
	Ground cinnamon or pomegranate seeds for sprinkling (optional)
	Melted chocolate for drizzling (optional)

In a blender or food processor, combine the almond paste, sugar, slivered almonds, milk, and almond extract and process just until blended.

Pour the mixture into a rectangular baking dish (Pyrex works well) and place in the freezer until partially frozen, about 2 hours. Remove from the freezer and use a fork to scrape the mixture into fine crystal shavings. Just keep scraping back and forth until you've reached the bottom of the dish. If some pieces seem too big, use the fork to smash them down a bit. You really can't mess this up.

Return the dish to the freezer until the mixture is again partially frozen, 30–60 minutes. (There is no perfect timing for this.) You do not want it to be rock hard. It should be starting to freeze along the edges and be frozen on top. Once again, remove the dish from the freezer and repeat the scraping process, then return it to the freezer. Repeat this scraping and refreezing two or three times until you have nicely sized crystal shavings.

Use a spoon or an ice-cream scoop to scoop the frozen granita into individual serving dishes. Store in the freezer until ready to serve. Let thaw for 2–3 minutes before serving. If you like, sprinkle on some cinnamon or pomegranate seeds before serving. A little melted chocolate drizzled on top never hurt, either.

Serves 6–8

peach & raspberry whole-wheat crostata

I love the rustic look and taste of this fruit-filled crostata. The whole-wheat flour gives the crust a nutty flavor and crumbly texture, while the turbinado sugar adds just enough sweetness. Make a few batches of the dough and reserve them in the freezer. That way, you can bake a crostata on short notice by just adding fresh fruit.

For the Crust

1	cup (5 oz/155 g) all-purpose flour
½	cup (2½ oz/75 g) whole-wheat flour
1½	teaspoons granulated sugar
	Kosher salt
¾	cup (6 oz/185 g) cold unsalted butter, cubed
1	large egg, beaten
1	tablespoon whole milk or soy milk

For the Filling

4–5	peaches, about 1½ lb (750 g) total weight, unpeeled, pitted and thinly sliced
1	pt (8 oz/250 g) raspberries or other berries
1	tablespoon granulated sugar
1	teaspoon fresh lemon juice
1	large egg, beaten
2	tablespoons turbinado sugar

To make the crust, in a food processor, combine the flours, sugar, and ½ teaspoon salt and process for 5 seconds. Add the butter and pulse until the butter is reduced to small pieces. Add the egg and milk and pulse just until moist clumps form.

Transfer the dough to a work surface, gather into a ball, and flatten into a disk. Wrap in plastic wrap and refrigerate for at least 1½ hours or up to 2 days. The dough will keep in the freezer for up to 3 months.

Preheat the oven to 400°F (200°C).

On a piece of parchment paper, roll out the chilled dough into a 12-inch (30-cm) round.

To make the filling, in a large bowl, stir together the peaches, raspberries, granulated sugar, and lemon juice. Spoon the fruit filling into the center of the dough, leaving a 1½-inch (4-cm) border. Gently fold the outer edges of the dough over the filling, pleating as needed. Brush the border with the egg wash and sprinkle with the turbinado sugar. Place the crostata, still on the parchment paper, on a baking sheet.

Bake until the crust is golden brown and the filling is bubbly, about 45 minutes. Serve warm.

Serves 8–10

chocolate chunk biscotti with lavender

This is one of my most popular recipes. It combines the light, dreamy flavors of lavender, vanilla, and chocolate, which together create a sublime cookie that will amuse your senses. To release its delicate flavors, rub the lavender between your fingertips, allowing the petals to break up and crumble. Divine!

½	cup (3½ oz/105 g) coconut sugar or firmly packed dark brown sugar
½	cup (4 fl oz/125 ml) olive oil
1	large egg
½	teaspoon vanilla extract
1½	cups (7½ oz/235 g) all-purpose flour
½	teaspoon baking soda
¼	teaspoon dried lavender, crushed between your fingertips
	Kosher salt
1	cup (5 oz/155 g) chocolate chunks (dark or milk chocolate)

Preheat the oven to 350°F (180°C). Line a baking sheet with parchment paper.

In a stand mixer fitted with the paddle attachment, beat together the coconut sugar, oil, egg, and vanilla on high speed for 1 minute. Reduce the speed to low, add the flour, baking soda, lavender, and a pinch of salt, and beat until a sticky dough forms, about 2 minutes. Stir in the chocolate chunks.

Use wet hands to divide the dough into 2 equal portions. Place the portions on the prepared baking sheet, spacing them about 3 inches (7.5 cm) apart. Shape each portion into a log about 4 inches (10 cm) in diameter and 10 inches (25 cm) long and flatten slightly with a wide spatula.

Bake until the logs are golden, about 25 minutes. Let cool for 10 minutes on the baking sheet. Reduce the oven temperature to 300°F (150°C). Use a wide spatula to peel off the parchment paper. Transfer the biscotti to a cutting board and use a sharp serrated knife to cut the logs crosswise into slices about ¾ inch (18 mm) thick or about 15 slices per log. Place the slices, cut side down, on the same parchment-lined baking sheet.

Bake until the biscotti are golden, about 10 minutes. Let cool completely on the pan on a wire rack. The biscotti will keep in an airtight container at room temperature for up to 1 month.

Makes about 30 biscotti

olive oil biscotti with hazelnuts & rose water

As I noted earlier, when it comes to cooking of any kind, less is often more, and this recipe is a testament to that philosophy. The combination of rose water and olive oil here results in the perfect little cookie. Accompany with freshly made coffee for the ultimate pairing.

1	large egg
1	cup (8 oz/250 g) sugar
1	teaspoon ground cinnamon
½	cup (4 fl oz/125 ml) olive oil
½	teaspoon rose water or orange flower water
½	cup (2½ oz/75 g) blanched and roasted hazelnuts
1¾	cups (9 oz/280 g) all-purpose flour
¼	cup (1½ oz/45 g) whole-wheat flour
¼	teaspoon baking soda
	Kosher salt

Preheat the oven to 350°F (180°C). Line a baking sheet with parchment paper.

In a stand mixer fitted with the whisk attachment, beat together the egg and sugar on medium speed for 1 minute. Add the cinnamon, oil, ¼ cup (2 fl oz/60 ml) water, and the rose water and beat until combined, about 2 minutes longer. Switch to the paddle attachment and beat in the hazelnuts, flours, baking soda, and a pinch of salt on low speed until evenly combined (or fold in with a spatula).

Use wet hands to divide the dough into 2 equal portions. Place the portions on the prepared baking sheet, spacing them about 3 inches (7.5 cm) apart. Shape each portion into a log about 4 inches (10 cm) in diameter and 10 inches (25 cm) long and flatten slightly with a wide spatula.

Bake until the logs are golden, about 25 minutes. Let cool completely on the pan on a wire rack. Be patient! Reduce the oven temperature to 300°F (150°C). Use a wide spatula to peel off the parchment paper. Transfer the biscotti to a cutting board and use a sharp serrated knife to cut the logs crosswise into slices about ¾ inch (18 mm) thick or about 15 slices per log. Place the slices, cut side down, on the same parchment-lined baking sheet.

Bake until the biscotti are golden, about 10 minutes. Keep an eye on them as they can burn quickly. Let cool completely on the pan on a wire rack. The biscotti will keep in an airtight container at room temperature for up to 1 month.

Makes about 30 biscotti

index

acknowledgments

To my amazing students, teachers, family, friends, and colleagues: Thank you for your constant encouragement and inspiration and for helping me do what I love to do.

Amy Marr: Thank you for your incredible patience and for believing in me from the start.

Andrea Burnett: You've been with me on this journey from the very beginning—thank you for teaching me as we go and for being so real.

Andrew Zuckerman: You talked about "my second book" even before we were done with the first. I am forever grateful to you.

To my unbelievably talented creative team, spearheaded by the delicious Ali Zeigler: Alison Attenborough, Hadas Smirnoff, Kate Sears, and Paige Hicks: it was a pleasure working with you, and I thank you for shining such positive energy on this project. To the rest of the Weldon Owen team: Amy Kaneko, Kelly Booth, Rachel Metzger, Marisa Kwek, and Stephanie McNamara—thank you for everything you've done.

Mom and Dad: You've always believed that your children were capable of everything and anything. And, because of you, we've all grown up to be strong, independent adults. Thank you for teaching us the value of happiness, selflessness, and family. We know how lucky we are to be your children.

To the Pekofsky and Kushner Bunch: Thank you for your constant love and support.

Lee and Murray: I feel so blessed to have come from a wonderful & loud family and to have become part of your wonderful & loud family!

Heidi, Jordana, and Matthew: No one will understand us the way we understand each other. You guys are seriously the best. Thanks for all your support, always.

Of course, I must mention my incredible nieces and nephews (because I promised them I would): Maayan, Eitan, Tal, Zac, Raya, Joseph, Leyla, Aviv, David, and Robert—I love you guys and I am thrilled about being your favorite aunt!

Milan, Emanuel, and Rafi: Of all the recipes I ever came up with, you are certainly the best. I love each one of you so much, it makes my heart want to explode with joy.

Jon: For all that you do for me, but more so, for the way you make me feel every single day. I love you beyond words.

weldonowen

1045 Sansome Street, Suite 100, San Francisco, CA 94111
www.weldonowen.com

THE NEW KOSHER

A WELDON OWEN PRODUCTION
Copyright © 2015 Weldon Owen, Inc.

Printed and bound in China by 1010 Printing, Ltd.

First printed in 2015
10 9 8 7 6 5 4 3 2 1

Library of Congress Cataloging-in-Publication
data is available.

ISBN 13: 978-1-61628-926-3
ISBN 10: 1-61628-926-0

Weldon Owen is a division of
BONNIER

WELDON OWEN, INC

President & Publisher Roger Shaw
SVP, Sales & Marketing Amy Kaneko
Finance Manager Philip Paulick

Associate Publisher Amy Marr
Associate Editor Emma Rudolph

Creative Director Kelly Booth
Art Directors Marisa Kwek, Alexandra Zeigler
Sr Production Designer Rachel Lopez Metzger

Production Director Chris Hemesath
Associate Production Director Michelle Duggan

Director of Enterprise Systems Shawn Macey
Imaging Manager Don Hill

Photographer Kate Sears
Food Stylists Alison Attenborough, Hadas Smirnoff
Prop Stylist Paige Hicks

ACKNOWLEDGMENTS

Weldon Owen wishes to thank the following people for their generous support in producing this book:
Kris Balloun, Sarah Putman Clegg, Gloria Geller, Elizabeth Parson, and Sharon Silva